BARRON'S EZ-101 STUDY KEYS

Jae K. Shim, MBA, Ph.D.
Professor of Business
   Economics
California State University,
Long Beach

and

Joel G. Siegel, CPA, Ph.D.
Professor of Accounting and
   Finance
Queens College of the City
University of New York

MACROECONOMICS

Second Edition

D1506658

All inquiries should be addressed to:
Barron's Educational Series, Inc.
250 Wireless Boulevard
Hauppauge, New York 11788
www.barronseduc.com

Library of Congress Catalog Card No. 2004059478

International Standard Book No. 0-7641-2923-6

Library of Congress Cataloging-in-Publication Data
Shim, Jae K.
   Macroeconomics / Jae K. Shim, Joel G. Siegel.—2nd ed.
      p. cm.—(Barron's EZ 101 study keys)
   Includes index.
   ISBN 0-7641-2923-6
   1. Macroeconomics. 2. Economic policy. 3. Economics. I. Siegel, Joel G.
II. Title. III. Series.

HB172.5.S5247 2005
339—dc22

                                                                    2004059478

PRINTED IN THE UNITED STATES OF AMERICA

9 8 7 6 5 4 3 2 1

CONTENTS

Theme 1   THE SCOPE OF ECONOMICS

*T*he objective of economics is to allocate scarce resources among competing activities in an efficient manner.

Economics attempts to tackle a wide variety of problems. It describes market processes, methods of trade, and how resources are allocated in an optimal way. It also deals with the conventional problems of inflation, unemployment, and international monetary affairs. Economic policy is concerned with finding solutions to these economic problems. Economic problems exist with scarce resources and unlimited wants.

Economics is divided broadly into two branches: microeconomics and macroeconomics. Microeconomics appraises individual economic units, including individuals and companies, while macroeconomics looks at the entire economy or major sectors of it.

The primary sectors are private and public. The former consists of households and businesses; the latter covers the government. Our U.S. economy is a capitalist, free-market one. Economic models may be used to simulate the economy in order to make predictions about the future.

INDIVIDUAL KEYS IN THIS THEME	
1	Objectives of economics
2	Microeconomics vs. macroeconomics
3	Private and public sectors
4	Economic systems
5	Economic theories and models
6	Economic policy

Key 1 Objectives of economics

OVERVIEW *Economics is a social science concerned with the study of how society chooses to use scarce resources to satisfy its unlimited wants.*

Economics is the study of how people and society end up choosing, with or without the use of money, to employ scarce production resources that could have alternative uses to produce various commodities and distribute them for consumption, now or in the future, among various persons and groups in a society. It analyzes the costs and benefits of improving patterns of resource allocation and attempts to tackle a wide variety of problems. It describes market processes, methods of trade, and how resources are allocated in an optimal way. It also deals with the conventional problems of inflation, unemployment, and international monetary affairs.

Economic policy is concerned with finding solutions to these economic problems.

Economic problems exist with scarce resources and unlimited wants.

Economic resources are the factors used in the production of goods. These are broken down broadly into two categories: Human resources such as labor and management and nonhuman resources such as land, capital, and technology.
   1. **Labor** includes management as well as working laborers employed in production activities.
   2. **Land** includes the surface area of the world plus all natural resources used in production such as water, forests, and minerals.
   3. **Capital** includes not only money but any capital or investment goods such as plant and equipment.
   4. **Technology** is the knowledge of how economic resources can be combined in a productive manner.

Key 2 Microeconomics vs. macroeconomics

OVERVIEW *There are two essentially different levels at which the study of economies takes place.*

Microeconomics is the study of the individual units of the economy—individuals, households, firms, and industries. It zeros in on such economic variables as the prices and outputs of specific firms and industries, the expenditures of consumers or households, wage rates, competition, and markets. The focus is on the trees, not the forest.

Questions that can be addressed by microeconomics include: What determines the price and output of individual goods and services? What are the factors that determine supply and demand of a particular good? How government policies such as price controls, subsidies, and excise taxes affect the price and output levels of individual markets?

Macroeconomics is concerned with the workings of the whole national economy or large sectors of it. It deals with national price, output, unemployment, inflation, and international trade.

Typical macroeconomic questions include: What determines national income and employment levels? What determines the general price level or rate of inflation? What are the policies that combat typical economic problems such as inflation, unemployment, and recession?

National income accounting provides aggregate measures of the value of the final goods and services produced in the economy, with **Gross Domestic Product (GDP), Net Domestic Product (NDP),** and **National Income (NI)** as different measures of the aggregate output (Keys 22 and 23).

Key 3 Private and public sectors

OVERVIEW *The economy consists of two primary sectors: the private sector and the public sector.*

The **private sector** encompasses all economic activities that are independent of government control (or outside the so-called public sector, carried on principally for profit. It also includes nonprofit organizations directed at satisfying private needs, such as private hospitals and private schools. Included are enterprises owned individually or by groups (such as corporations with numerous stockholders) as well as the self-employed.
- In national income accounting, the private sector adds the total net value to the economy by nongovernment producers of goods and services. This includes not only the output of profit and nonprofit private corporations, proprietorships, and partnerships, but also that of self-employed individuals such as farmers, dentists, and the like.
- The private sector accounts for about 88 percent of gross national product in the United States.

The **public sector** covers all economic activities—mostly services—that are carried out directly by government agencies (or outside the private sector), largely for the public benefit rather than for profit. Included is the entire machinery of government offices and agencies on the local, state, and national levels, and all the various enterprises they support (police and fire protection, military payrolls, highway maintenance, public education, and so on).
- In national income accounting, the public sector adds the value to the economy by government agencies consisting primarily of services performed by government employees.
- In the United States, with but few exceptions (such as ships built in navy yards and guns made in army arsenals), the goods used in the public sector are produced in the private sector. For example, a bomber used by the air force or a municipal fire truck represent output of the private sector even though they are used in the public sector.
- For this reason, the contribution of the public sector to national output—about 12 percent of gross national product—is less than government purchases of goods and services (about 22 percent), which includes both government payrolls and purchases from private contractors.

Key 4   Economic systems

OVERVIEW   *An economic system refers to a particular system of organization for the production, distribution, and consumption of products and services people use to achieve a certain standard of living.*

All societies and nations do not agree on the optimal way to address these economic issues. For example, the U.S. economy uses a capitalist or free-market system while the former Soviet economy is a socialist or planned economy.

Every economic system must answer the following questions:
- What goods and services should be purchased?
- How many of these goods and services should be produced?
- How should these goods be produced?
- For whom should these goods be produced?

There are three basic types of economic systems. They are:
1. A **traditional economic system** relies upon custom, habit, social mores, and tried-and-true methods for achieving economic goals; technology is primitive; changes are slow and production is undertaken in the same way as last year and the year before. Tradition and the status quo are perpetuated. Examples include the feudal system of the Middle Ages and today's underdeveloped countries.
2. A **command economic system** relies on public ownership and centralized control of the basic means of production. Service limitations are placed upon individual choice when such choices conflict with government-determined economic priorities. Economic plans and activities are under the control of an economic authority such as a central planning board. Heavy use is made of governmental directives, the assumption being that the government is in the best position to decide what economic choices and policies are most beneficial for the economy and its component parts. The economic questions are solved by government planning. Individual decision-making plays only a small role in setting economic policy. Both socialistic and communistic nations are examples of command economies.
3. A **capitalistic** or **market economic system** emphasizes private ownership, individual economic freedom, competition, the profit motive, and the price system in the achievement of economic goals. Each economic unit decides what choices and policies are

best for it, the theory being that in encouraging the drive for individual economic self-interest, the outcome proves to be in the overall best interests of society because of the strong incentives for efficiency, productivity, and satisfaction of consumers. The "what," "how," "how much," and "for whom" questions are primarily solved by a system of free markets.

The U.S. economy has a relatively strong capitalistic orientation (although it also has a moderate dose of command and, therefore, is most properly described as a "mixed capitalistic" economic system). There is a mixture of private and public enterprise and decision making. The solutions to the preceding questions result from government planning and regulation as well as the market system.

Key 5   Economic theories and models

OVERVIEW *Economists build theories, or simplified models of the real world to better explain the interrelationships between many economic variables.*

Economic theories, or more often called **principles or laws,** can be positive or normative.

Positive theory deals with the economy as it is rather than as it should be, with the consequences of a change in economic policy or conditions. It is descriptive in the sense that it only describes past events and relationships among variables and there are no value judgments involved as to what the economy should be.

Normative theory involves value judgments—what prices, minimum wages, and government policies dealing with, say, inflation and federal deficit ought to be. It is prescriptive in the sense that it prescribes some choice among alternative economic policies.

An **economic model** is a simplified representation of an economy, or some part of an economy.
- It yields predictions about behavior that can be tested against statistical evidence. This process of explaining economic events by building and testing models is called positive economics.
- It is used, for example, to forecast gross domestic product or national income or investment from one year to the next, and to project a major change in interest rates or government spending.

Key 6 Economic policy

OVERVIEW *Economic policy is concerned with finding solutions to economic problems.*

While policy makers use economic theory to help them, they must go beyond it as well. They must consider the cultural, social, legal, and political aspects of an issue if they are to formulate a successful policy. In the end, making economic policy involves making value judgments such as those we will explore when we look at the conflict between unemployment and inflation in Key 70. An economist has no special claim over anybody else to making these judgments.

Policy makers have at their command two broad classes of policies with which to affect the economy:
- **Monetary policy** is controlled by the Federal Reserve System (the Fed). The instruments of monetary policy are changes in the stock of money; changes in the interest rate—the discount rate—at which the Fed lends money to banks; and some controls over the banking system.
- **Fiscal policy** is under the control of the Congress, and usually is initiated by the executive branch of the government. The instruments of fiscal policy are tax rates and government spending.

One of the central facts of policy is that the effects of monetary and fiscal policy on the economy are not fully predictable, neither in their timing nor in the extent to which they affect demand or supply. These two uncertainties are at the heart of the problem of stabilization policy.

Stabilization policies are monetary and fiscal policies designed to moderate the fluctuations of the economy—in particular, fluctuations in the rates of growth, inflation, and unemployment. A list of economic policy goals that economic policy makers feel are important in the United States would probably look like this:
1. **Price stability:** In recent years this has meant checking inflation.
2. **Full-employment:** In recent years most economists would take this to mean keeping the unemployment rate down around 4 percent.
3. **Economic growth:** Continued growth in the standard of living for the average citizen.
4. **Environmental standards:** More control over the pollution and wastes that our production processes produce and impose on the environment.

5. **Economic security:** Provision of an adequate standard of living for those unable to work, either because of age, illness, or other handicaps beyond their control, or because there are simply not enough jobs for all who want them.

6. An **equitable tax burden:** People, especially the middle-income groups, have shown increasing concern because our tax system typically favors those in higher income brackets, who are in a position to take advantage of loopholes in the tax laws to avoid or greatly reduce their "fair share" of the tax burden.

7. **Economic freedom:** The idea that businesses, consumers, and workers should be given much freedom in their economic activities.

Economic experience has suggested, however, that goals 1 and 2 may not be compatible, and that there seems to be trade-off between the achievement of one at the expense of the other. The same may be true of goals 3 and 4, and goals 4 and 7.

Goals 2, 3, and 5 all seem compatible in the sense that if we achieve 2 and 3, we will very likely enhance economic security, goal 5.

With respect to goal 6, some would argue that some of the so-called loopholes are important to spur risky business ventures. They argue that without tax breaks for these enterprises there would be fewer of the enterprising activities essential to economic growth and full employment (goals 2 and 3). They would contend that goal 6, therefore, may not be compatible with goals 2 and 3.

Theme 2 BASIC CONCEPTS IN ECONOMICS

*A*n examination must be made as to the effect one economic variable has on another, such as how quantity demanded changes as price changes. These relationships may be expressed in mathematical or graphical terms. Marginal (rate of change) analyses are also informative including marginal revenue, marginal cost, marginal profit, marginal product, and marginal propensity to consume and to save.

Production possibilities have to be looked at to get maximum use out of scarce resources. The supply and demand relationships determines the price of a good or a service. The market equilibrium between price and quantity is the point where the demand and supply curves intersect.

An interrelationship exists between macroeconomic factors some being positively correlated while others are being negatively correlated.

Key 7 Functions, graphs, and equations

OVERVIEW *In economics it is important to talk about relationships between different economic quantities.*

There is a relationship between the price of a good (or service) and the quantity that people will purchase.

There are two basic types of analysis: **Mathematical** and **graphical.**

The expression $Y = f(X)$ (Read Y is a function of X) means that the value of Y depends on the value of X. For example, the quantity of a commodity that people will purchase depends upon the price for which the commodity can be purchased.

This expression tells us nothing, however, about the nature of the relationship. It can mean that as X increases, Y increases; or it can mean that it will decrease. $Y = f(X)$ means merely that there is a relationship so that for every value of X, there is a value of Y.

If, however, we say, for example:
$$Y = 4X + 5$$

we have stated a specific hypothesis or idea and we have given content to that relationship. As the value of X increases by 1, the value of Y increases by 4. We can, in fact, know the value of Y for every value of X.

Consider the following functional relationship: $Y = 2X + 2$ where X stands for the amount of fertilizer used and Y for the amount of the resulting crop.

We can make a table or schedule of this relationship showing the value of Y for a few values of X:

If $X =$	Then $Y =$
0	2
1	4
2	6
3	8
4	10

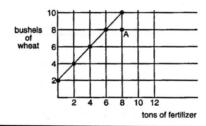

Each point of the preceding grid (not just the ones emphasized) represents a value of X and a value of Y. For example, the point labeled A represents $X = 8$, $Y = 8$. To graph this equation, we simply plot several points consistent with the equation on the graph and draw a line through these points. Each point on the line shows the given value of X (tons of fertilizer) and the corresponding value of Y.

Note that in mathematics, it is usual to use Y as the dependent variable and X as the independent variable and to graph the relationship with X on the horizontal axis and Y on the vertical axis. Sometimes, however, economists represent the dependent variable on the horizontal axis and the independent variable on the vertical axis. An example of this is in supply and demand analysis for which price (the independent variable) and quantity (the dependent variable) are graphed respectively on the vertical and horizontal axis.

KEY FIGURE 2

Key 8   Marginal measures

OVERVIEW   *Economic decisions are often based on such marginal measures as output, revenue, cost, or profit.*

In microeconomics, **marginal revenue** must equal **marginal cost** in order for profit to be maximized. In a discrete range of activity, **marginal revenue** is equivalent to **incremental revenue.**

- **Marginal Revenue (MR)** is the rate of change of total revenue with respect to quantity sold. Marginal revenue indicates to a firm how total sales will change if there is a change in the quantity sold of a firm's product.
- **Marginal Cost (MC)** is the change in total cost associated with a unit change in quantity. For example, the marginal cost of the 500th unit of output can be calculated by finding the difference in total cost at 499 units of output and total cost at 500 units of output. It is, therefore, the additional cost of one more unit of output and is calculated as

$$MC = \text{change in total cost/change in quantity}$$

Marginal Cost is also the change in total variable cost associated with a unit change in output. This is because total cost changes, whereas total fixed cost remains unchanged. It may also be thought of as the rate of change in total cost as the quantity (Q) of output changes and is simply the first derivative of the total cost (TC) function. Thus,

$$MC = dTC/dQ$$

- **Marginal Profit** is marginal revenue less marginal cost.
- **Marginal Product (MP)** is the additional output obtained by adding one extra input (e.g., additional oranges picked by adding one more laborer).
- **Marginal Revenue Product (MRP)** is marginal revenue times the marginal product (e.g., if MR is $1 and MP is 10 units, then MRP is $10).

Marginal Propensity to Consume (MPC) is the fraction or proportion of any change in income which subsequently is spent for consumption (Key 32). In other words, the MPC is the ratio of a change in consumption to a change in income or:

$$MPC = \frac{\text{change in consumption}}{\text{change in income}} = \frac{\Delta C}{\Delta Y}$$

Marginal Propensity to Save (MPS) is the fraction of any change in income that is saved; that is, the MPS is the ratio of the change in saving to the corresponding change in income:

$$MPS = \frac{\text{change in saving}}{\text{change in income}} = \frac{\Delta S}{\Delta Y}$$

Since, by definition, all income that does not go for consumption is saved, it follows that $MPC + MPS = 1$.

Key 9   Production possibility frontier

OVERVIEW   *The basic economic problem is the combined existence of unlimited human wants and limited resources.*

Scarcity is a fact of life. When there is the conflict between scarce resources and unlimited wants, choice is inescapable. In other words, scarcity implies choice that has a cost, or more exactly opportunity cost.

The scarcity and choices inherent in the economy can be represented graphically. Assume that an economy can produce two goods, **weapons** (*W* goods) and **foods** (*F* goods). Although there is a maximum the economy can produce, choices can be made between the two alternatives.

Assuming full employment of all available resources and efficient use of known technologies, it is possible to plot all possible production combinations of these two goods that this economy could produce over a given time period, say a year. The result is known as a **Production Possibility Curve (PPC)** and is illustrated in Figure 1 by the curve *FW*.

KEY FIGURE 1

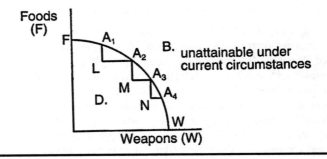

A **PPC**, also called a **Production Possibility Frontier** or a **Production Transformation Curve**, is a graphic representation of all the possible combinations of goods and services that can be produced when all resources are fully and efficiently employed.

In Figure 1, the F goods (in physical units) are measured on the vertical axis, while the W goods (also in physical units) are measured on the horizontal axis.

Any point on FW shows maximum feasible combinations of F goods and W goods that can be produced with the resources available. B, which lies outside the curve, is not a feasible or attainable combination. D, which lies inside the curve, is feasible but not desirable, since more could be produced with available resources.

Scarcity, or goods unattainable with the available resources and given technologies, is illustrated by points to the right of the PPC. Points inside the FW curve, while attainable, imply either under-utilized resources or inefficiencies in production. For example, with the recession in 1991, the United States operated well inside its PPC. Over time, with increases in the available resources (e.g., growth in the labor force and additions to the capital stock through net investment) and with new technologies, the production possibilities curve will shift to the right.

Choice is illustrated by the need for society to select one combination to produce and consume. Opportunity cost is represented by the slope of the PPC; that is, producing more F goods, for example, necessitates the transfer of resources away from the production of the W goods produced.

The curvature of the PPC illustrates the assumption of increasing **opportunity cost.** If all resources are not equally well suited for the production of both types of goods, then increasing the production of one type of good by equal amounts will entail sacrificing larger amounts of the other good. In other words, the opportunity cost rises.

Moving down the PPC from combination $A1$ to combination $A4$ requires a transfer of resources away from the production of F goods to that of W goods. In each instance, the gain in W goods production is the same: $A3N = A2M = A1L$. The loss in F goods production, however, is increasing: $A4N < A3M < A2L$. This is due to specialization of resources, and in this case, the increasing need to use resources less suited for the production of W goods as the level of W goods produced rises. In the face of scarcity, people have devised a variety of ways to improve the productivity of resources including:
- Development of substitute resources.
- Specialization of labor.
- Utilization of economies of scale.

Key 10 Supply and demand

OVERVIEW *Demand is the quantity of a good or service that consumers are willing and able to purchase at various prices during a period of time.*

Demand is a schedule of amounts that will be purchased at various prices.

Supply is the amount of a good or service that producers are willing and able to offer to the market at various prices during a specified period of time.

The **price** of a product and the quantity demanded are inversely (negatively) related, i.e., the lower the price, the higher the quantity demanded.

With a price decrease, new buyers will enter the market. The good will be cheaper relative to other goods, and is substituted for them (substitution effect).

With lower prices, individuals buy more of all goods than they formerly purchased (income effect).

The determinants of demand are variables that affect the amount of a product purchased. For example, with consumer income, there are:
- **Normal goods** that are commodities for which demand is positively (directly) related to income, e.g., steak, clothes, leisure time.
- **Inferior goods** that are commodities for which demand is negatively (inversely) related to income, e.g., potatoes, bread.

There is also consumer taste and preference plus prices of closely related goods, such as:
- Substitutes: If products A and B are substitutes, a price increase in A will generate an increase in the demand for B. For example, butter and margarine.
- Complements: If products A and B are complements, a price increase in A will generate a decrease in the demand for B. For example, bread and jelly.

Price expectations play a part, as well. Do consumers expect prices to rise or fall?

The **demand schedule** is a relationship between the prices of a commodity (vertical axis) and the quantity demanded at the various prices (horizontal axis), holding other determinants of the quantity demanded constant. A movement along an existing demand curve occurs when the price is changed (E below).

A **shift** in the curve itself occurs when any of the determinants change. The graph illustrates an increase in demand, i.e., the demand curve shifts from D to $D1$. Such an increase in demand for commodity A (a shift in the demanded schedule outward or to the right) can be caused by:

1. A favorable change in the tastes and preferences of consumers toward commodity A (e.g., resulting from a successful advertising campaign).
2. An increase in consumer income, if A is a normal good.
3. A decrease in consumer income, if A is an inferior good.
4. An increase in the price of commodity Y, if Y is a substitute for A.
5. A decrease in the price of commodity X, if X is a complement for A.
6. The expectation of future price increases.

KEY FIGURE 1

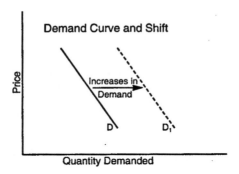

A decrease in demand for commodity A (a shift in the demand schedule inward or to the left) can be caused by the opposite of the factors listed above.

The **Law of Supply** is the price of the product and the quantity supplied that are positively (directly) related. The determinants of supply are the variables that affect the amount supplied, as follows:
- Production prices.
- Technology.
- Prices of other goods.

- Price expectations.
- Taxes and subsidies.

The supply schedule is a relationship between the price of a good (vertical axis) and the quantity supplied to the market (horizontal axis) at each price. A change in the price of a commodity is represented as a movement along the supply schedule.

A shift in the supply curve itself is caused by a change in the determinants. The graph illustrates an increase in supply, which shifts the line from S to $S1$.

KEY FIGURE 2

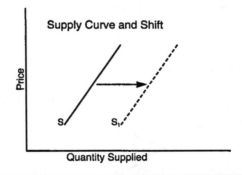

Supply Curve and Shift

An increase in supply for commodity A (a shift in the supply schedule to the right) can be caused by changes in the determinants, as follows:
- A decrease in a factor of the production price.
- An improvement in technology.
- A decrease in the demand for another commodity (B), inducing firms to divert resources from the production of B to A.
- The expectation of future price decreases.
- A decrease in taxation of a good or an increase in subsidization.

A decrease in supply can be caused by the opposite of the above determinants.

Market equilibrium can take place only at a price where the quantities supplied and demanded are equal (Key 11).

Key 11 Market equilibrium

OVERVIEW   *The market is the interaction of buyers and sellers of a commodity brought into contact with one another to engage in purchases and sales of economic goods (e.g., items that individuals prefer more of than less of).*

Equilibrium between price and output is the point at which the demand and supply curves intersect. Figure 1 illustrates the concept of market equilibrium, e.g., the intersection of a supply and demand curve.

KEY FIGURE 1

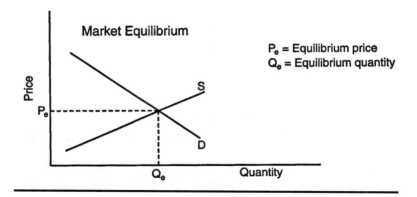

At the point of intersection of the supply and demand curves, anyone wishing to purchase the good at the market price can do so. This results in an automatic, efficient rationing system of supply and demand caused by the nature of market forces.

At any price higher than the equilibrium intersection of the supply and demand curves, the quantity that producers will want to go on supplying will exceed the quantity that consumers will want to go on demanding. Downward pressure on price will then result as some of the excess sellers undermine the going price.

Similarly, a price lower than the equilibrium price will tend to generate shortages and to generate production to meet upward pressure from bids of excess buyers.

The following represents the impact on equilibrium of shifts in supply and demand:

1. An increase in supply (demand held constant) will cause the price to decrease and the quantity supplied to increase.
2. A decrease in supply (demand held constant) will raise the equilibrium price and lower output.
3. An increase in demand (supply held constant) will increase prices and increase output.
4. A decrease in demand (supply held constant) will lower price and quantity demanded.
5. Simultaneous shifts in supply and demand and their resulting effects on equilibrium can be summed up as follows:

- An increase (decrease) in demand and supply will cause the quantity of output to increase (decrease), but the effect on the equilibrium price is indeterminable.
- An increase (decrease) in demand and a decrease (increase) in supply will cause the equilibrium price to increase (decrease) but the effect on output is indeterminable.

Key 12 Relationships among
macroeconomic variables

OVERVIEW *Many macroeconomic variables are inter-related. Some relationships are directly related, while others are inversely related.*

Greater output is associated with high levels of employment. It therefore follows that increases in real economic growth would be associated with reductions in the rate of unemployment.

Okun's Law suggests that an annual 2.5 percent increase in real GNP above trend growth results in a 1 percent decrease in the rate of unemployment (Key 20).

The **Phillips Curve** is the curve that represents a statistical inverse relationship between unemployment and inflation. Every point on the curve denotes a different combination of unemployment and inflation. A movement along the curve reflects the reduction in one at the expense of a gain in the other.

The dilemma posed by the curve is that the economy must accept inflation in order to achieve full employment or to accept a high unemployment rate to control inflation (Key 70).

Key 13 Aggregate demand and
supply

OVERVIEW *The key analytical apparatus for under-standing how the macroeconomy ticks is Aggregate Supply (AS) and Aggregate Demand (AD).*

Aggregate supply describes how much real GDP businesses would produce and sell given prices, costs, and market conditions.

Aggregate demand is determined by the total spending in an economy by households, businesses, and governments. It represents the total real output that would be bought at every price level.

AS and AD curves have the same shapes as the familiar macroeconomic supply and demand curves, as shown in Figure 1.

Aggregate demand slopes down in part because consumers are able to stretch their dollar incomes and wealth further at a lower price level.

Similarly, AS slopes up in the short run because businesses face some dollar-fixed costs (such as those in wage contracts); in such a circumstance, firms will both produce more goods and raise prices somewhat as demand increases. They can make a higher profit at higher goods prices and are thus willing to produce more.

The overall macroeconomic equilibrium, determining both aggregate price and output, comes where the AS and AD curves intersect.

KEY FIGURE 1

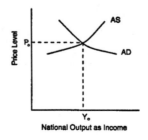

National Output as Income

Theme 3 FUNDAMENTAL MACROECONOMIC CONCEPTS

M oney is used to buy goods and services and serves as a medium of exchange. The economy basically consists of households, businesses, and government. Businesses consist of three types: Sole proprietorships, partnerships, and corporations.

The circular flow of income consists of payments and receipts for goods and services. Businesses sell goods and services to households buying them. The business cycle is the expansionary and contractionary trend in the economy. Key economic issues include employment, inflation, and growth.

INDIVIDUAL KEYS IN THIS THEME	
14	Money
15	Prices and resource allocation
16	Firms, households, and government
17	Circular flow
18	Business cycle
19	Unemployment
20	Unemployment and full employment
21	Inflation

Key 14 Money

OVERVIEW   *Money is anything that functions as a generally accepted medium of exchange and as a standard unit of account in terms of which goods and services can be compared.*

There are three main kinds of money (listed in order of present-day importance): bank money, currency (coins and paper money), and commodity money.

- **Bank money,** consisting largely of demand deposits, credit/charge cards, travelers checks, and other kinds of interest-bearing checking accounts, make up about three-fourths of the total U.S. money supply. Currency accounts for nearly all the rest.
- **Commodity money** (gold, shells, cows, tobacco, etc.) is still used in some parts of the world but not in the developed nations. Whereas commodity money may have intrinsic value (as gold coins obviously do), currency and bank money are, in fact, liabilities; that is, they are claims on the government and on banks respectively. That these claims are generally accepted as payment for physical goods represents an act of faith.

Money has traditionally been defined by four functions:

1. Serving as a **medium of exchange** is far and away the most important function of money. When you buy something, you pay for it with money rather than barter with some other merchandise.
2. Being a **store of value** means that money retains its value over time. You would hardly be willing to accept money in payment if you didn't think that someone else would accept the money from you tomorrow.
3. Saying that money is the **unit of account** just means that prices are quoted in dollars and cents. (A grocery could post a sign showing that three apples cost two oranges.)
4. **Standard of deferred payment** means that when someone owes a debt, the payment is specified in terms of money.

Key 15 Prices and resource allocation

OVERVIEW *Price is a mechanism by which goods and services are rationed and resources or factors of production are allocated.*

Competitive pricing distributes the limited supply of goods and services to those who desire them the most.

Along with helping to decide *For Whom*, market prices signal changes in *What* shall be produced and in *How* goods and services shall be produced.

Any one market cannot help solve the *What, How,* and *For Whom*.

Each market's interdependence with other goods and services produce the general-equilibrium system of prices.

Key 16 Firms, households, and government

OVERVIEW *Our mixed economy is like a three-legged stool.*

One leg represents households; the second, businesses; and the third, government. The first two constitute the private sector of the economy. The third is the public sector, which is primarily government.

Households:
- You and I are part of the household segment of the private sector. So, too, are some 80 million families.
- Households are the ultimate suppliers of the economy's inputs of human resources and the major purchasers of its outputs of goods and services.

Businesses:
- Businesses, of which there are more than 15 million, including farmers and professional people, make up the second major group within the private sector. This group accounts for most of the society's production of goods and services.
- A firm is a business organization that brings together and coordinates the factors of production—capital, land, labor, and entrepreneurship—for the purpose of supplying goods or services.

There are three basic forms of business organizations:
1. A **sole proprietorship** is a business owned by one individual. Of the three forms of business organizations, sole proprietorships are the greatest in number. The advantages of this form are:
   a. No formal charter required.
   b. Minimal organizational costs.
   c. Profits and control not shared with others.
   The disadvantages are:
   a. Limited ability to raise large sums of money.
   b. Unlimited liability for the owner.
   c. Limited to the life of the owner.
2. A **partnership** is similar to the sole proprietorship except that the business has more than one owner. Its advantages are:
   a. Minimal organizational effort and costs.
   b. Free from governmental regulations.
   c. Each partner's share of income is reported on his or her personal income tax return.

Its disadvantages are:
  a. Unlimited liability for the individual partners.
  b. Limited ability to raise large sums of money.
  c. Dissolved upon the death or withdrawal of any of the partners.
  d. Each partner is legally responsible for the acts of other partners.

There is a special form of partnership, called **limited partnership,** where one or more partners (but not all), have limited liability (up to their investment) to creditors in the event of failure of the business. Limited partners are not involved in daily activities. The return to limited partners is in the form of income and capital gains. Often, tax benefits are involved.

3. A **corporation,** also called a *C corporation,* is a legal entity that exists apart from its owners, better known as stockholders. Ownership is evidenced by possession of shares of stock. In terms of types of businesses, the corporate form is not the greatest in number, but the most important in terms of total sales, assets, profits, and contribution to national income. The advantages of a corporation are:
  a. Unlimited life.
  b. Limited liability for its owners.
  c. Ease of transfer of ownership through transfer of stock.
  d. Ability to raise large sums of capital.

Its disadvantages are:
  a. Difficult and costly to establish, as a formal charter is required.
  b. Subject to double taxation on its earnings and dividends paid to stockholders.
  c. Strict governmental regulation.
  d. Significant bookkeeping.

4. **Subchapter S corporation:** a form of corporation whose stockholders are taxed as partners. It distributes its income directly to shareholders; avoids corporate income tax while enjoying the other advantages of the corporate form. To qualify as an S corporation, a corporation must:
  a. Have fewer than 75 shareholders; none may be nonresident foreigners.
  b. Have only one class of stock.
  c. Properly elect Subchapter S status.

Government:
  • Government uses public expenditures and taxes to influence the level of employment and business activity and to purchase public goods (e.g., bridges, highways).

- It provides a central banking authority to control the availability of money and credit.
- It regulates the factors of production such as capital and labor, to create and maintain competition and discourage monopolistic activities.
- It exerts influence on the redistribution of income through such means as taxation, large-scale borrowing, and transfer payments.

Key 17 Circular flow

OVERVIEW *The circular flow is the continual flow of income—in the form of payments and receipts for goods and services—in an economy.*

The **circular flow concept** is actually an abstract, oversimplified model of the economic transactions constantly taking place. For example,
1. Households buy goods and services. The payments for these become the income of the firms producing the goods and services.
2. To produce them in the first place, the firms must pay the factors of production: rent (land), wages (labor), interest (capital), and profit (entrepreneur). These payments, in turn, are the source of household income, spent on the consumption of goods and services. When all income is spent on consumption, the circular flow is complete.

From the microeconomic viewpoint, circular flow describes the market for goods and the market for factors of production, with both households and businesses operating as buyers in one market and sellers in the other.

From the macroeconomic viewpoint, circular flow describes national income, which will remain the same so long as withdrawals (in form of saving, taxes, and spending for imports) are exactly equal to input (investing spending, government spending, selling goods abroad).

In both cases, the **static equilibrium** is the theoretical rather than actual.

Figure 1 presents the **simplified model** (with no government) of national output as a flow of income and expenditure. The public, as owners of economic resources, sell its resources to producers in the resource markets.

From the viewpoint of the public, the sale of these resources generates money income; from the viewpoint of producers, the purchase of economic resources represents a cost of production. Producers utilize the resources they purchase to make goods and services that, in turn, are sold to the public via product markets. The public's source of income to make these purchases is, of course, the money income obtained as resource suppliers.

From the public's viewpoint the purchases of goods and services are **expenditures;** from the producer's viewpoint these same dollar flows are **revenues.**

Both the clockwise flow of economic resources and final goods and services and the counterclockwise flow of money incomes and dollar expenditures for final goods and services are simultaneous and repetitive.

KEY FIGURE 1

The Circular Flow Operation of a Monetary Economy

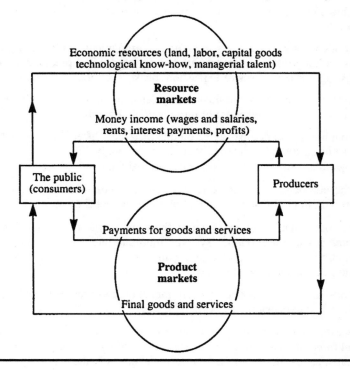

Economic resources (land, labor, capital goods technological know-how, managerial talent)

Resource markets

Money income (wages and salaries, rents, interest payments, profits)

The public (consumers)

Producers

Payments for goods and services

Product markets

Final goods and services

Key 18 Business cycle

OVERVIEW *The business cycle is the regular pattern of expansion (recovery) and contraction (recession), an aggregate economic activity around the path of trend growth, which affects on growth, employment, and inflation.*

The **business cycle** is a pulse common to most sectors of economic life and to diverse countries.

In cycles we see movements in GDP, unemployment, prices, and profits, although the movements are not so regular and predictable. We distinguish the phases of expansion, peak, recession, and trough.

A first clue to the source of business cycles is found in the amplitude of fluctuations of investment or durable capital goods.

Although most economists agree on this fact, they differ in their emphasis upon external or internal factors. Increasingly, however, they lean toward a synthesis of external and internal factors.

On the one hand, importance is attached to fluctuations in population growth, in gold discoveries, and in political events or wars.

On the other hand, economists stress the way that these external factors interact with the economic system. Important interactions include the multiplier and the acceleration principle, which bring in dynamic rates of change as well as levers.

The business cycle tends to have an impact on corporate earnings, cash flow, and expansion.

Forecasting the business cycle is still inexact. Today, the most successful forecasters use medium-to large-scale computer models, based on statistical estimates, to forecast future changes in the economy.

RECESSION:

Recession means a sinking economy. Unfortunately, there is no consensus definition and measure of recession. In general, it means that the economy is shrinking in size and the number of jobs being lost outnumbers jobs being created. Here are three primary ways economists define a recession:

    1. Three or more straight monthly drops of the Index of Leading Economic Indicators are generally considered a sign of recession.

2. Two consecutive quarterly drops of Gross Domestic Product (GDP) signals recession.

3. Consecutive monthly drops of durable goods orders that most likely results in less production and increasing layoffs in the factory sector.

Key 19 Unemployment

OVERVIEW *Unemployment is the nonavailability of jobs for people able and willing to work at the prevailing wage rate. It is an important measure of the economic health, since full employment is generally construed as a desired economic goal.*

Full employment exists when all individuals willing to work at prevailing market wages are employed at tasks appropriate for their skills. For a policy perspective, full employment exists when the unemployment rate is approximately 4 percent to 7 percent. Normal workings of the market will result in about a 6 percent level of unemployment due to job turnover.

The **unemployment rate** is the number of unemployed workers divided by total employed and unemployed who constitute the labor force.

The types of unemployment are:
1. **Frictional unemployment,** which is the amount of unemployment due to the normal workings of the labor market, e.g., approximately 4 percent at "full" employment, according to policy definition. This acknowledges that there will be some unemployment at any given time due to workers changing jobs, or temporary layoffs. It differs from structural unemployment in that it is generally short in duration, lasting only as long as it takes to find a new job. However, delays may be caused by imperfect knowledge of job opportunities, lack of mobility, or the need for retraining.
2. **Structural unemployment** exists when aggregate demand is sufficient to provide full employment, but the distribution of the demand does not correspond precisely to the composition of the labor force, e.g., NASA engineers who were left unemployed at the end of the race to the moon. It is unemployment resulting from changes in the overall economy, principally changes in population, government policies, technology, and consumer tastes, but not from the ups and downs of the business cycle (which can cause cyclical unemployment). For example, a declining birth rate in recent decades resulted in increasing unemployment among teachers; reduced government spending for defense caused massive unemployment in defense-related industries; and the fashion for longer hair among men and boys led to many unemployed or underemployed barbers.

3. **Cyclical unemployment** is caused by a downturn in the business cycle, specifically by lack of demand for labor. Generally the lowest-paid, least-skilled workers are the first to be laid off, but in a prolonged period of business contraction layoffs gradually affect all groups. Hardest hit are workers in capital goods industries, whose volume of input fluctuates most widely with business-cycle fluctuations.

4. **Seasonal unemployment** occurs periodically owing to seasonal variations in particular industries. It is particularly evident in jobs affected by weather, either in terms of the ability to perform any work at all (construction, agriculture) or in terms of consumer demand for the end-product (Christmas ornaments, air conditioners, summer and winter resorts).

Economic cost of unemployment can be measured in terms of the foregone output, i.e., the gap between potential GDP if we had it, and actual GDP.

Noneconomic costs of unemployment are equally important and refer to the individual and the social degradation implicit in the loss of meaningful employment and income.

UNEMPLOYMENT INDICATORS: UNEMPLOYMENT RATE, INITIAL JOBLESS CLAIMS, AND HELP-WANTED INDEX

Many analysts look to the unemployment rate as being the most important.

- The **unemployment rate** is the number of unemployed workers divided by total employed and unemployed who constitute the labor force. The **median duration of unemployment** is an indication of how serious unemployment is. Both statistics are released by the Department of Labor.

- **Weekly initial claims** for unemployment benefits are another closely watched indicator along with the unemployment rate to judge the jobless situation in the economy.

- The **help-wanted advertising index** tracks employers' advertisements for job openings in the classified section of newspapers in 50 or so labor market areas. The index represents job vacancies resulting from turnover in exiting positions such as workers changing jobs or retiring and from the creation of new jobs. The help-wanted figures are seasonally adjusted. The help-wanted advertising figures are obtained from classified advertisements in newspapers in major labor markets. *Note:* An increase in employment, a decrease in initial jobless claims, and a decrease in unemployment are favorable for the economy and the stock market; the opposite situation is unfavorable. The help-wanted index is inversely related to unemployment. When help-wanted advertisements increase, unemployment declines, while a decline in help-wanted advertisements is accompanied by a rise in unemployment. The effect of unemployment on the economy is summarized in the figure below.

UNEMPLOYMENT EFFECTS:

1. **Less tax revenue.** Fewer jobs means lower income tax to the state and nation, which means a bigger U.S. government deficit and forces states to make cuts in programs to balance their budgets.
2. **Higher government costs.** When people lose jobs, they often must turn to the government for benefits.
3. **Less consumer spending.** Without a job, individuals can't afford to buy cars, computers, houses, or vacations.
4. **Empty stores.** Retailers and homebuilders can't absorb lower sales for long. Eventually they have to lay off workers and, in more serious shortfalls, file for bankruptcy.
5. **Manufacturing cuts.** The companies that make consumer products or housing materials are forced to cut jobs, too, as sales of their goods fall.
6. **Real estate pain.** As companies fail and as individuals struggle, mortgages and other bank loans go unpaid. That causes real estate values to go down and pummels lenders.

Key 20 Unemployment and full employment

OVERVIEW *Full employment is the availability of work at prevailing wage rates for all persons who desire it, but does not mean 100 percent employment. There always is some unemployment, because of job changes, seasonal factors, and the like.*

Most economists define **full employment** as meaning that a given percentage of the work force is employed. Until the mid-1970s this figure was 96 percent, meaning that when full employment was achieved, unemployment was no higher than 4 percent (Key 19).

By the early 1980s many economists agreed that in view of increased structural unemployment this was an unrealistic goal and needed to be revised to 6 to 7 percent unemployment.

Most economists (but not all) consider full employment a highly desirable goal for any economy, because it often is equated with maximum utilization of economic resources: land, labor, capital.

To maintain aggregate full employment, the government may enact monetary and fiscal policies to encourage business expansion. However, these policies also stimulate price inflation.

Okun's Law describes the relationship between changes in the rate of economic growth (measured by changes in real GDP) and changes in the unemployment rate. This law is attributed to Arthur Okun, chairman of the Council of Economic Advisors under President Johnson.

The law states that for every 2½ percentage points of growth in real GDP above a trend rate that is sustained for a year, the unemployment rate declines by 1 percentage point. This means that the economy must continue to grow considerably faster than its trend (long-term average) rate to achieve a substantial reduction in the unemployment rate.

For example, suppose that the trend rate of growth is 3 percent per year and the unemployment rate is currently 9 percent. How many years would it then take to return to a target rate of, say, 6 percent unemployment? The answer pretty much depends on how fast the economy is able to grow during the recovery period.

Assume that the growth rate of potential output is 3 percent per year. One possible path to achieve the target is for output to grow at 5½ percent per year for three years. On this path, each year the economy is growing 2½ percent above the trend, and thus each year it takes 1 percentage point off the unemployment rate.

Key 21 Inflation

OVERVIEW *Inflation means a general rise in the price level. When inflation is present, a dollar today can buy less than a dollar could in the past.*

Although the causes of inflation are diverse, a frequent source of inflationary pressure is the excess demand for goods and services that pulls product prices upward—**demand-pull inflation.** Rising wages and material costs may lead to the upward pressure on prices—**cost-push inflation.**

Furthermore, excessive spending and/or heavy borrowing due to a budget deficit by the federal government can be inflationary. All of these sources may be intermingled at a particular point in time, making it difficult to pinpoint the cause for inflation.

The types of inflation are:
1. **Demand-pull inflation.** This is a situation in which prices keep rising, triggered by a continuing high demand for goods. This is created when "too much money chases too few goods." It can be controlled by Federal Reserve actions that curb the money supply and a fiscal policy that cuts government spending, raises taxes, and reduces budget deficits.
2. **Cost-push inflation.** It is also called **price-wage spiral** or **wage-push inflation.** This is when consumer and industrial prices keep rising because of a continuing demand for higher wages. Powerful labor interests negotiate increasingly high wage settlements to enable the workers they represent to meet rising consumer prices. Industries then raise prices to meet their higher labor costs (and usually a little more, to increase profits), leading workers in turn to demand still higher wages.

Also, to be fair and balanced, powerful businesses can decide to increase their profits by raising prices, thus causing workers to seek wage increases to meet their higher costs.

In extreme cases, the government may intervene and impose wage controls, either by urging unions and management to hold wage increases within a particular "guideline" or, if the situation is considered an emergency, by setting mandatory limits.

In general, inflation tends to redistribute wealth haphazardly without regard to social goals. It also impairs a nation's efficiency and growth.

SIDE EFFECTS OF DEFLATION:

Deflation has often had the side effect of increasing unemployment in an economy, since the process often leads to a lower level of demand in the economy. Other downside effects include possible pay cuts and more expensive repayment of consumer debts. The upside of falling prices: Mild deflation would assure working people (at least those who fend off pay cuts) of steadily rising real wages.

Theme 4 MEASURING ECONOMIC
ACTIVITY

*T*here are many measures of macroeconomic activity. A major barometer of economic conditions is the Gross Domestic Product (GDP), which measures the value of all goods and services. Net national product is GDP adjusted for capital consumption allowances. National income is how much income is earned by resource suppliers. Disposable income is personal income less personal taxes.

An index number is a measure of relative value compared to a base quantity. It is used to compare the changes in economic phenomena over time. Four types of indexes are price, quantity, volume, and a combination of these. A simple price index is the relationship of one price to another for a specific commodity. A weighted price index looks at the price relationships among several commodities.

The GDP Deflator is a weighted-average of the price indexes of the current period.

INDIVIDUAL KEYS IN THIS THEME	
22	Gross Domestic Product
23	Other national income measures
24	Simple index numbers
25	Bundled (weighted) index numbers
26	Measures of inflation—price indexes
27	Index number problems
28	Real and nominal measures
29	Measures of money supply
30	Measuring unemployment

Key 22 Gross Domestic Product (GDP)

OVERVIEW *Gross Domestic Product (GDP) measures in dollars the value of all final goods and services produced within the boundaries of the United States and is the nation's broadest gauge of economic health.*

Gross Domestic Product (GDP) only includes the values of goods and services earned by a nation within its boundaries. Thus, it includes only the income derived from factories *within* the country (and not without), whether by domestic or foreign-owned sources.

There are two approaches to the GDP:
1. Suppose that we want to measure the market value of an automobile. One way to do this is to look at how much the consumer pays for the automobile. Although this is the most straightforward way to measure the automobile's market value, it is not the only way it can be done.
2. Another, equally valid way is to add up all of the wage, interest, rental, and profit incomes generated in the production of the automobile. As pointed out in the circular flow model (Key 16), the amount that the automobile producer receives for this car is equal to its profit (or loss) on the car plus the amount it pays the workers and other resource owners who contributed their resources to its production. Thus, if we add up all of the wage, interest, rental, and profit incomes resulting from the production of the automobile, the result is the same as if we determine how much the consumer pays for the automobile.

There are also ways to measure the market value of the output of the economy as a whole. Or, put differently, ways of looking at GDP:
- The **expenditures approach,** which regards GDP as the sum of incomes derived from the production of this year's total output.
- The **income approach,** which regards GDP as the sum of wages, interest, rent, and profits received by the factors of production.

Because both of these approaches are valid, it follows that GDP can be viewed as either the total expenditure on this year's total output or as the total income stemming from the production of this year's total output. In other words,

$$
\begin{array}{ccc}
\text{The total} & & \text{The total income} \\
\text{expenditure on} & = \text{GDP} = & \text{stemming from} \\
\text{this year's total} & & \text{the production of} \\
\text{output} & & \text{this year's total} \\
& & \text{output}
\end{array}
$$

This is an **identity;** the left-hand side of this equation must equal the right-hand side.

It is important to understand both the income and the expenditures approaches to GDP.

Because the categories of expenditure previously described include all possible types of spending on final goods and services, their sum equals GDP. In other words,

GDP = personal consumption expenditures (C) + gross private domestic investment (I) + government purchases of goods and services (G) + net exports (NX).

The sum of the five types of income described above (plus depreciation and indirect business taxes) equals gross national product, or

GDP = compensation of employees + rent + interest + proprietors' income + corporate profits + depreciation + indirect business taxes.

The limitations of GDP are that it
- Fails to reveal anything about the quality of life, value of leisure time, costs of growth such as crime and pollution, and value of education and health care.
- Excludes many nonmarket activities, including homemakers' activities and "underground economy."

Key 23 Other national income
measures

OVERVIEW *There are several important national income accounting concepts that can be derived from GDP.*

National income accounting is the accounting system for macroeconomics that provides various income concepts. It is a necessary step in learning how macroeconomic variables—such as the economy's total output, the price level, the level of employment, interest rates, and others—are determined.

As a measure of total output, GDP tends to provide a somewhat exaggerated picture because it fails to make allowance for that part of current output necessary to replace the capital goods used up in producing the current GDP.

Net Domestic Product (NDP) is GDP adjusted for capital consumption allowances (or total economy-wide depreciation charges); NNP measures the total annual output that the entire economy can consume without impairing its capacity to produce in future years.

National Income (NI) defines how much income is earned by resource suppliers for their contributions to the GDP. National income is calculated by subtracting indirect business taxes from NDP and it measures the total income that all factors of production earn for their current contributions to the productive process.

National income can be calculated just as well by adding up the sum of total of compensation to employees, rental income, interest income, and profits.

Personal Income (PI) is calculated by subtracting from national income those three types of income earned but not received and by adding income received but not currently earned:

National Income–
    Social Security Contributions
    Corporate Income Taxes
    Retained Earnings
       + Transfer Payments = Personal Income

Disposable Income (DI) is simply personal income less all kinds of personal taxes (personal income taxes, personal property taxes, sales taxes, and inheritance taxes).

Personal saving (S) can be thought of as a residual; that is, it is the amount of disposable personal income remaining after personal consumption expenditures.

National income accounting formulas are as follows:

1. Gross Domestic Product (GDP) = C + I + G + NX
2. Net Domestic Product (NDP)
   - NDP = GDP – Capital Consumption Allowance (Depreciation)
   - NDP = C + Net Investment + G + NX
3. Net Investment = I – Depreciation
4. National Income (NI)
   - NI = NDP – Indirect Business Taxes
   - NI = Sum of Factor Payments
5. Personal Income (PI)
   - PI = NI – Social Security Contributions – Corporate Income Taxes – Retained Earnings + Transfer Payments
   - PI = Household Income
6. Disposable Income (DI)
   - DI = PI – Personal Taxes
   - DI = Take Home Household Income
   - DI = Consumption Expenditures + Personal Savings + Interest Payments to Businesses
   - DI = NI – Corporate Profits – Taxes (personal, corporate, and Social Security) + Personal Dividend Receipts + Interest Paid by Government + Transfer Payments by Government and Businesses to Households
7. Personal Savings (S)
   - S = DI – C

Where   C   = household consumption spending
        I   = gross investment
        G   = government spending
        NX = foreign net export spending

Key 24 Simple index numbers

OVERVIEW *The two principal kinds of formulae used for index numbers are simple (unweighted) and weighted.*

A simple form of **price index** is the ratio of one price to another for a specific commodity. It is simple to calculate the index number, using the formula

$$I = \frac{P_n}{P_1} \times 100$$

where I = index number, P_n = price in any chosen year, and P_1 = base-year price. (This formula is known as a simple average of relatives.)

Consider a gallon of milk, with a base-year price of $1. If milk goes up to $1.10 in Year 2 (the following year), to $1.15 in Year 3, $1.40 in Year 4, the index numbers would be 110 for Year 2, 115 for Year 3, and 140 for Year 4. One also might say that the price of milk had risen 10 percent from the base period to Year 2, 15 percent to Year 3, and 40 percent to Year 4.

A simple average works well for one commodity but falls down as soon as several commodities (milk, meat, cranberries) or, for a quantity index, different units of measure (liters, kilograms, meters) enter the picture.

For the former, it distorts matters because the different foods mentioned have unequal importance in the total budget, a fact that becomes even more obvious if the items are not food but automobiles, milk, and funerals. In that case, a conversion to a common measure would be required.

The same drawback holds true for a **simple aggregative average,** in which the prices of all the commodities under consideration are added and divided by the price they commanded in the base year. A single item that rises by a considerable sum will make the overall average rise too much, thereby distorting the picture.

These drawbacks can be avoided in part by working with a weighted average; of these, one of the most commonly used is the **Laspeyres Index** (Key 25).

Key 25 Bundled (weighted) index
numbers

OVERVIEW *A simple average works well for one commodity but is deficient as soon as several commodities or different units of measure enter the picture.*

For example, it distorts matters because the different foods mentioned have unequal importance in the total budget, a fact that becomes even more obvious if the items are not food but automobiles and funerals. These drawbacks can be avoided in part by working with a weighted average.

Both the **Producer Price Index (PPI)** and **Consumer Price Index (CPI)** are price indexes that compare the current and base year cost of a basket of goods of fixed composition. If we denote the base year quantities of the various goods by q^i_o and their base year prices by p^i_o the cost of the basket in the base year is $\sum p^i_o q^i_o$ where the summation $(\sum)$ is over all the goods in the basket.

The cost of a basket of the same quantities but at today's price is $\sum p^i_o q^i_o$ where p^i_t is today's price.

The CPI or PPI is the ratio of today's cost to the base year cost or,

$$\text{Consumer or producer price index} = \frac{\sum p^i_t q^i_0}{\sum p^i_0 q^i_0} \times 100$$

This is a so-called **Laspeyres,** or base-weighted, price index.

The GDP deflator by contrast uses the weights of the current period to calculate the price index. Let q^i_t be the quantities of the different goods produced in the current year.

$$\text{GDP deflator} = \frac{\text{GDP measured in current prices}}{\text{GDP measured in base year prices}}$$
$$= \frac{\sum p^i_t q^i_t}{\sum p^i_0 q^i_t} \times 100$$

This is known as **Paasche,** or current weighted, price index.

Comparing the two formulae we see that they differ in that q^i_o, or the base year quantities, appears in both the numerator and denominator of the CPI and PPI formula, whereas q^i_t appears in the formula for the deflator.

Key 26 Measures of inflation—price indexes

OVERVIEW *Price indices are used to measure inflation. They are, therefore, used to measure costs of living, price-level changes, and real GDP. They are the Consumer Price Index, Producer Price Index, GDP Deflator, and Employment Cost Index.*

The price index (PI) for Year t is shown as follows:

$$PI = \frac{\text{Cost of Basket in Year } t}{\text{Cost of Basket in Base Year}} \times 100$$

The rate of inflation in Year t is:

$$\frac{PI \text{ (Year } t) - PI \text{ (Year } t-1)}{PI \text{ (Year } t-1)} \times 100$$

MEASURES OF INFLATION:

Price indices are designed to measure the rate of inflation of the economy. Various price indices are used to measure living costs, price level changes, and inflation. They are:

1. **Consumer Price Index.** The Consumer Price Index (CPI), the best-known inflation gauge, is used as the cost-of-living index, which labor contracts and social security are tied to. The CPI measures the cost of buying a fixed bundle of goods (some 400 consumer goods and services), representative of the purchase of the typical working-class urban family. The fixed basket is divided into the following categories: food and beverages, housing, apparel, transportation, medical care, entertainment, and other. Generally referred to as a **"cost-of-living index,"** it is published by the Bureau of Labor Statistics of the U.S. Department of Labor. The CPI is widely used for escalation clauses. The base year for the CPI index was 1982-1984 at which time it was assigned 100.

2. **Producer Price Index.** Like the CPI, the PPI is a measure of the cost of a given basket of goods priced in wholesale markets, including raw materials, semifinished goods, and finished goods at the early stage of the distribution system. The PPI is published monthly by the Bureau of Labor Statistics of the Department of Commerce. The PPI signals changes in the general price level, or the CPI, some time before they actually materialize. (Since the PPI

does not include services, caution should be exercised when the principal cause of inflation is service prices.) For this reason, the PPI and especially some of its subindexes, such as the index of sensitive materials, serve as one of the leading indicators that are closely watched by policy makers. It is the one that signals changes in the general price level, or the CPI, some time before they actually materialize.

3. **GDP Deflator.** The index of inflation used to separate price changes in GDP calculations from real changes in economic activity. The Deflator is a weighted average of the price indexes used to deflate the GDP so true economic growth can be separated from inflationary growth. Thus, it reflects price changes for goods and services bought by consumers, businesses, and governments. Because it covers a broader group of goods and services than the CPI and PPI, the GDP Deflator is a very widely used price index that is frequently used to measure inflation. The GDP deflator, unlike the CPI and PPI, is available only quarterly, not monthly. It is published also by the U.S. Department of Commerce.

4. **Employment Cost Index.** The most comprehensive and refined measure of underlying trends in employee compensation as a cost of production. It measures the cost of labor and includes changes in wages and salaries and employer costs for employee benefits. ECI tracks wages and bonuses, sick and vacation pay, plus benefits such as insurance, pension, and Social Security and unemployment taxes from a survey of 18,300 occupations at 4,500 sample establishments in private industry and 4,200 occupations within about 800 state and local governments.

Key 27 Index number problems

OVERVIEW *An index number is a measure of relative value compared with a base quantity for the same series.*

In a time series in index form, the base-period value is often set at 100, and data for other periods are expressed as percentages of the value in the base period.

Index numbers are used primarily to compare the changes in various economic phenomena over time (year to year, month to month, or even hour to hour in the case of stock indexes).

The U.S. Federal government publishes numerous indices concerning the overall economy, among them the CPI and PPI (Key 26).

Indices are published by, among others, industries, private foundations, state and local governments, university bureaus of business research, and the United Nations Statistical Office. There are four principal kinds of indices:
- Price.
- Quantity, such as the Federal Reserve Board Index of Industrial Production.
- Value, such as the Total Retail Sales Index.
- Special-purpose, most often involving some combination of the other three (such as the Forbes Index, combining production, money turnover, employment, department store sales).

A **composite index** is one made up of other indexes.

All indexes have three features in common.
1. Every index number has a base period, which is assigned a given value (usually 100, but 10 in the case of Standard & Poor's Composite Stock Price Index, 50 in the New York Stock Exchange's Composite Index, and so forth).
2. All indexes measure a representative selection of items—a given list of products, employment in certain industries, and the like. This selection is but a sample from which more general information is inferred and, obviously, the inference can be only as good as the sample and the procedures used in obtaining it.
3. Every index is computed according to some statistical formula, so that the index numbers for different time periods are comparable. The two principal kinds of formulae used are simple (unweighted) and weighted.

A simple form of price index is the ratio of one price to another for a specific commodity (Key 24).

A simple average distorts matters because the different foods mentioned have unequal importance in the total budget, a fact that becomes even more obvious if the items are not food but automobiles, milk, and funerals.

These drawbacks can be avoided in part by working with a weighted average; of these, one of the most commonly used is the **Laspeyres Index** (Key 25).

Key 28 Real and nominal measures

OVERVIEW   *Nominal measures are ones such as a price quoted for a commodity, security, currency, or other item that has not been actively traded and that, therefore, has no current market price.*

Normally a **nominal price** is based on the most recent market price available, or on the price for a comparable item. Real measures are the ones adjusted for price change (inflation).

Nominal wages are earnings regarded in terms of their face value rather than their purchasing power.

Real wages are the amounts of workers' earnings (the so-called money wage) adjusted to take purchasing power into account. A real wage is calculated by dividing an index number of general prices into the money wage.

$$R = \frac{M}{PI} \times 100$$

where R is the real wage, M is the money wage, and PI is the price index number.

In practice, if prices rise faster than money wages, the real wage declines; if money wages decline more slowly than prices (as during a business slump), real wages rise.

Nominal GDP measures the value of output in a given period in the prices of that period, or, as it is sometimes put, in current dollars. Thus 1993 Nominal GDP measures the value of the goods produced in 1993 at the market prices that prevailed in 1993.

Nominal GDP changes from year to year for two reasons:
1. The physical output of goods changes.
2. Market prices change.

As an extreme and unrealistic example, one could imagine the economy producing exactly the same output in two years, between which all prices have doubled. Nominal GDP in the second year would be double Nominal GDP in the first year, even though the physical output of the economy has not changed at all.

Real GDP measures changes in physical output in the economy between different time periods by valuing all goods produced in the two periods at the same prices, or in constant dollars.

Real GDP is now measured in the national income accounts in the prices of 1996, which means that in calculating real GDP, today's physical output is multiplied by the prices that prevailed in 1996 to obtain a measure of what today's output would have been worth had it been sold at the prices of 1996.

Key 29 Measures of money supply

OVERVIEW *Money supply is the level of funds available at a given time for conducting transactions in an economy.*

The **Federal Reserve System** can influence the money supply through its monetary policy measures. There are many measures of the money supply, designated by the symbols M1, M2, M3, and L. Of these four measures, M1 is the narrowest, or least inclusive, and L is the broadest, or most inclusive.

1. M1 is a broadly used measure of money supply. It covers currency in circulation, checkable deposits (demand deposits, NOW, share draft, and other accounts), and traveler's checks.

Because checkable deposits are readily convertible into cash, M1 is frequently referred to as the **"basic money supply."**

2. M2 = M1 + medium-range money, such as:
    Savings (time) deposits.
    Repurchase agreements (overnight).
    Money market mutual fund shares.
    Eurodollars (overnight).

3. M3 = M2 + wide-range money, such as:
    Large-denomination time deposits.
    Term repurchase agreements.
    Term Eurodollars.

4. L = M3 + liquid and near-liquid assets, such as:
    Short-term Treasury securities.
    High-grade commercial paper.
    Bankers' acceptances.

Key 30 Measuring unemployment

OVERVIEW *The nonavailability of jobs for persons able and willing to work at the prevailing wage rate. Unemployment is an important measure of the economic health, since full employment is generally considered a highly desirable goal.*

The Bureau of Labor Statistics, which regularly compiles statistics on unemployment, defines unemployed persons as any civilians over 16 years of age who, during a given week, had no employment but were available for work, and had been actively seeking a job (through an employment office, interviews, and so forth) within the past four weeks; were waiting to return to a job from which they had been laid off; or were waiting to report to a new paid job within 30 days.

They are considered employed if they performed work as paid civilians for one or more hours during the previous week. Those employed 35 or more hours a week are considered full-time workers, and those employed one to 34 hours a week are part-time.

Unpaid workers are counted if they worked 15 or more hours in a family business.

Also counted as employed are those with jobs who were temporarily absent for various reasons, including a strike. Discouraged workers, who are not seeking jobs because they feel they will not be able to find one, are not counted among the unemployed.

Unemployment statistics, which are reported monthly, are adjusted to account for seasonal variation.

The unemployment rate can be calculated as follows:

$$\frac{\text{The number of unemployed workers}}{\text{Total labor force}} \times 100$$

An unemployment rate of 4 percent was long considered normal and in fact was defined as "full employment." By the mid-1980s, however, most economists felt this figure was unrealistic and that 6 to 7 percent unemployment would more accurately reflect an economy at "full employment." (Keys 19 and 20)

Theme 5   EQUILIBRIUM OUTPUT AND INCOME

C onsumption is the most important element of total spending and is primarily determined by disposable income. The marginal propensity to consume is the proportion of any change in income that is later used for consumption.

Another major component of spending is the investment in housing, plant, and equipment. Investment is undertaken to make a profit. The amount of investment spending is tied into the interest rate. Investment has a multiplier effect on production volume.

Aggregate demand is the sum of consumption and investment spending in a two-sector model, while aggregate supply is the amount of goods and services available for sale. The equilibrium level of income (output) is the level at which aggregate supply equals aggregate demand—that is, where the total output of goods and services equals the total quantity demanded.

Key 31 The 45-degree line graph

OVERVIEW *The 45-degree line is a valuable reference line on which all points have the same value on the horizontal and vertical axes.*

In the **consumption-disposable income** graph, the 45-degree line tells us whether consumption at each level of income is above, at, or below income.

In Figure 1, at Point *B,* consumption equals income ($4,000). Point *A* is above the 45-degree line, so consumption is above income; Point *C* is below this line, so consumption is below income.

In the **Aggregate Demand (AD)/Aggregate Supply (AS)** diagram, equilibrium occurs where the total spending curve intersects the 45-degree line (where AD = AS) (Key 35).

KEY FIGURE 1

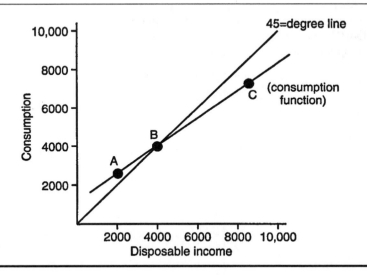

Key 32 Consumption and marginal
propensity to consume

OVERVIEW   *The largest component of total spending is consumption.*

The most important determinant of the level of consumer spending is income—in particular disposable income. **Consumption** and **disposable personal income** are directly and closely related. That fraction of any given total amount of disposable income spent for consumption purposes is called the **Average Propensity to Consume (APC):**

$$APC = \frac{\text{consumption}}{\text{income}} = \frac{C}{Y}$$

However, just because consumers spend a certain fraction of a given income does not guarantee they will consume the same fraction of any change in income that might occur.

The fraction or proportion of any change in income subsequently spent for consumption is called the **Marginal Propensity to Consume (MPC).** In other words, the MPC is the ratio of a change in consumption to a change in income or:

$$MPC = \frac{\text{change in consumption}}{\text{change in income}} = \frac{\Delta C}{\Delta Y}$$

Key 33 Saving and marginal
propensity to save

OVERVIEW *Saving is the difference between income and consumption. Consumption depends on income and therefore, saving depends on income.*

That fraction of total disposable income saved is called the **Average Propensity to Save (APS)**:

$$APS = \frac{saving}{income} = \frac{S}{Y}$$

However, just because consumers save a certain fraction of a given income does not guarantee they will save the same fraction of any change in income that might occur.

The fraction of any change in income that is saved is called the **Marginal Propensity to Save (MPS)**; that, is, the MPS is the ratio of the change in saving to the corresponding change income:

$$MPS = \frac{change\ in\ saving}{change\ in\ income} = \frac{\Delta S}{\Delta Y}$$

Since, by definition, all income that does not go for consumption is saved, it follows that $APC + APS = 1$ and $MPC + MPS = 1$.

Economists assume the values of MPC and MPS to be constant—not only because this is consistent with statistical evidence but also because it greatly simplifies their economic analysis. Exhibit 1 illustrates the relationship between consumption, saving, and income. Note that $APC + APS = 1$ and $MPC + MPS = 1$.

The following table illustrates the relationship between consumption and income—the concepts of APC and MPC.

(1)	(2)	(3)	(4)	(5)	(6)	(7)
Disposable income (Y)	Consumption (C)	Saving (S) (1)–(2)	APC (2)/(1)	APS (3)/(1)	MPC ΔC/ΔY	MPS ΔS/ΔY
$ 8,000	$ 9,200	−$1,200	1.15	−0.15	0.70	0.30
10,000	10,600	− 600	1.0	−0.06	0.70	0.30
12,000	12,000	0	1.00	0.00	0.70	0.30
14,000	13,400	600	0.96	0.04	0.70	0.30
16,000	14,800	1,200	0.93	0.07	0.70	0.30
18,000	16,200	1,800	0.90	0.10	0.70	0.30
20,000	17,600	2,400	0.88	0.12	0.70	0.30
22,000	19,000	3,000	0.86	0.14	−	−

KEY FIGURE 2

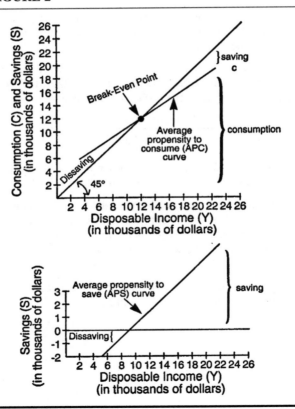

Key 34 Investment

OVERVIEW *The second large component of spending is investment in housing, plant, and equipment.*

The primary economic forces that determine investment are the revenues produced by investment (primarily influenced by the state of the business cycle), the cost of investment (determined by interest rates and tax policy), and the state of expectations about the future.

Because the determinants of investment depend on highly unpredictable future events, investment is the most volatile component of aggregate spending.

An important relationship is the **investment demand schedule**, connecting the level of investment spending and the interest rate. When firms' choices of investment projects are driven by profits, this will lead to a downward-sloping investment demand curve. A higher interest rate will lead firms to cancel some investment projects.

In making investment decisions, the **real interest rate** is particularly relevant. The real rate of interest corrects the more familiar nominal interest rates for the rate of inflation. Thus: real interest rate–nominal interest rate–rate of inflation.

Because the people and reasons involved in savings and investment are different, and because markets do not quickly and automatically channel savings to investors, there may well be a prolonged mismatch between them. This can result in output being away from its potential, and in faster or slower price increases.

The **accelerator principle** is a proposition that net investment in capital goods depends upon changes in the level of GDP. If aggregate demand increases, the economy, operating at full capacity, will have to undertake additional investment in order to produce an increase in GDP. Thus,

$$\text{Net investment} = \text{accelerator} \times \text{change in GDP}$$

and hence

$$\text{Accelerator} = \frac{\text{Net investment}}{\text{Change in GDP}}$$

The **accelerator** is estimated by statistical methods.

Key 35 Determination of equilibrium output and income—a two-sector model

OVERVIEW *Aggregate supply is the quantity of goods and services producers make available for sale and is equal to the money income received by the owners of the factors of production. Aggregate demand is the sum that buyers plan to spend on output.*

The **equilibrium level of income** (output) is the income (output) level at which aggregate supply equals aggregate demand; that is, where the total output of goods and services equals the total quantity of goods and services demanded.

Aggregate demand consists of **consumption (C)** and **investment spending (I)** in a two-sector model.

Assuming that there is a constant level of planned investment spending, and that household aggregate consumption is positively related to the receipt of personal income, there is only one level of income where aggregate supply Y equals aggregate demand $C + I$.

Example: The aggregate supply and demand data are presented in Table 1 and Figure 1. The equilibrium level of income remains at $520. At supply levels below $520, consumption plus investment spending exceeds what is being offered for sale. At supply levels above $520, consumption plus investment spending is less than output.

Aggregate Supply (Output/Income)	Consumption	Investment	Aggr. Demand (C + I)
$480	$450	$50	$500
500	460	50	510
520	470	50	520
540	480	50	530
560	490	50	540

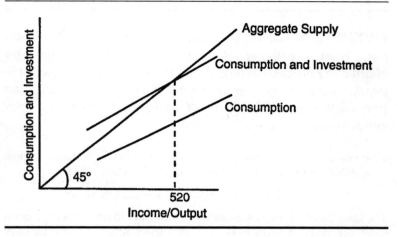

Key 36 The multiplier

OVERVIEW *Investment has a multiplier effect on output. When investment changes, there is an equal primary change in national output. But as the income receivers in the capital-goods industries get more earned income, they set into motion a whole chain of additional secondary consumption spending and employment.*

If people always spend about two-thirds of each extra dollar of income upon consumption, the total of the multiplier chain will be:

$$1 + 2/3 + (2/3)^2 + \ldots = 1/(1 - (2/3)) = 1\tfrac{1}{2} = 3$$

The **multiplier** works upward or downward, amplifying either increases or decreases in investment. The simplest multiplier is numerically equal to the reciprocal of the MPS, or equivalently, to

$$1/(1 - MPC) = 1/MPS$$

This result occurs because it always takes more than a dollar of increased income to bring forth a dollar of increased saving.

Example: Suppose that the MPS is one-third. If so, a \$1 billion increase in intended investment will increase equilibrium income by $1\tfrac{1}{2}$ billion; that is, by \$3 billion.

Since MPS is less than one, the multiplier must be greater than one. In other words, an increase in intended investment of \$1 will result in an increase in national income of more than \$1. As noted above, this means that national income is relatively sensitive to changes in intended investment.

Moreover, since the multiplier is the reciprocal of the MPS, the smaller the MPS, the higher the multiplier—and the more sensitive is national income to changes in intended investment.

This result has important implications for public policy. For example, because our system of taxes and transfer payments tends to increase the marginal propensity to save out of national income, the destabilizing effect of a sharp change in investment expenditures frequently is reduced.

Key 37 Saving and investment

OVERVIEW *There is an alternative, useful formulation of the equilibrium condition that aggregate demand is equal to output. In equilibrium, planned investment equals saving. This condition applies only to a two-sector economy in which there is no government and no foreign trade.*

The **equilibrium level of income** can be found by a saving/investment (leakages/injection) approach as well as by equating aggregate supply output and aggregate demand $(Y = AD)$.

Saving is a leakage from the circular flow. **Investment spending** is an injection into the circular flow that offsets a saving leakage.

The equilibrium level of income occurs where planned saving (total leakages) equals planned investment (total injections).

We can express this by starting with the basic equilibrium condition, which states that in equilibrium, $Y = AD$. If we subtract consumption from both Y and AD, we realized that $Y - C$ is saving and $AD - C$ is planned investment. In symbols,

$$Y = AD$$

$$Y - C = AD - C$$

$$S = I$$

Thus, the condition $S = I$ is merely another way of stating the basic equilibrium condition.

Example: In Table 1, planned saving, the difference between consumption and the income obtained from production, is added to the data originally given in Key 35. Planned saving equals planned investment at the $520 equilibrium level of income. Investment injections equals saving leakages.

Table 1

Aggregate Supply (Income/Output)	Consumption	Saving	Investment
$480	$450	$30	$50
500	460	40	50
520	470	50	50
540	480	60	50
560	490	70	50

KEY FIGURE 1

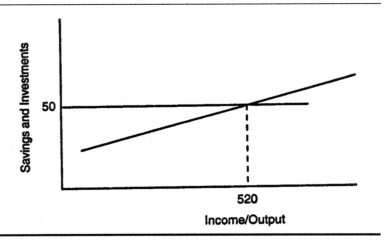

Key 38 Net exports

OVERVIEW *Net exports is the difference between exports and imports. It is a component of aggregate demand of the economy.*

By and large, the size and direction of **net exports** do not exert a strong influence on the overall level of economic activity in the United States. This is due mainly because net exports represent a very small percentage of the GDP.

The factors determining the size of the difference between our exports and our imports include such things as tariff and quota policies, foreign exchange rates and currency restrictions, the relative prices of foreign goods versus domestic goods, the health of the international economy, levels of income in foreign nations, and the attitudes of nations toward foreign trade.

As with government spending, there are no guiding economic principles for predicting the size and the direction of change in net exports as these relate to changes in income and the GDP.

Because of this and because net exports constitute such a small proportion of GDP (typically less than 1 percent), the foreign trade sector is often ignored for purposes of analyzing fluctuation in GDP, income, and employment.

Theme 6   FISCAL POLICY

*D*isposable income is affected by the tax rate. Taxes are a source of government spending that depend on public needs and priorities. A change in spending can magnify changes in real aggregate income. A change in income equals the expenditure multiplier times the change in spending. A change in taxes has less of an affect on the macroeconomy than an equal change in government spending.

Under the balanced budget multiplier hypothesis, an increase in government spending and taxes results in an increase in gross national product by the same amount. Hence, the balanced budget multiplier is 1.

Fiscal policy is a program directing government spending and taxes to keep actual GDP near the potential full employment GDP. Inflation reduces the purchasing power and wealth of individuals. It can cause a reduction in the output of goods and services.

Key 39 Taxation and the
consumption function

OVERVIEW *Changes in personal income taxes (T) have an impact upon the size of disposable income (Y_d).*

By definition, **disposable income** is income (Y) minus taxes. That is, $Y_d = Y - T$.

The **consumption function** is:
$$C = a + b\,(Y - T) = a + b\,Y_d$$

Saving (S) is $Y - C$. Therefore, $S = Y - C = Y - [+ b(Y - T)]$
$$\text{So, } S = -a + (1 - b)\,Y - b\,T.$$

In general, an increase in tax rates will also tend to reduce consumption (C) and saving (S) at each level of income. Conversely, a decrease in tax rates will tend to increase consumption and saving at almost every level of income.

Key 40 Government spending

OVERVIEW *One major component of aggregate demand stems from government. The other three come from households, businesses, and international activity.*

The size and type of government spending depends primarily on public needs and social priorities.

The volume of government spending, both for goods and services and for transfer payments, tends to be independent of profit expectations. Once the bare minimum government essentials are taken care of, the level of government spending is primarily a function of social-political-economic considerations.

Government spending may or may not be closely tied to the amount of tax revenues and to the current level of economic activity; moreover, there is not an immutable economic law or guiding set of principles that governs changes in the level of government spending.

In this sense, at a given time, government spending can be thought of as being partly autonomous—that is, independent of the size of the GDP and income levels.

Key 41 Expenditure multiplier

OVERVIEW *The expenditure multiplier is a principle that states that changes in total spending can bring about magnified changes in real aggregate income. The expenditure multiplier is thus the same as the investment multiplier, except that the independent variable is broadened to include total spending rather than just investment spending.*

The **expenditure multiplier concept** is expressed by the equation: Change in income = expenditure multiplier × change in spending (Note that the variables are expressed in *real,* not nominal, terms).

The expenditure multiplier emphasizes the idea that any change in spending, whether by households, businesses, or government, and whether for consumption or for investment, can have a multiplier effect on income.

The multiplier is given by the formula

$$\text{Expenditure multiplier} = \frac{\text{Change in income}}{\text{Change in spending}}$$

$$= 1/MPS = 1/(1 - MPC)$$

Example: Assume that the MPC = .25. What is the effect of a \$1 billion increase in aggregate spending? The multiplier is $1/.75 = 1.33$, that is, equilibrium income will increase by \$1.33 billion.

Key 42 Tax multiplier

OVERVIEW *Tax changes are first encountered at the income side of the model, rather than at the demand for goods and services side.*

A $1 change in taxes is going to lead to a $1 change in income rather than to a $1 change in aggregate spending. The $1 change in taxes is subject to the MPC, so consumption is changed by $.90 (assuming an MPC of .9); therefore, the initial change in aggregate spending is $.90 rather than $1.

Any change in taxes has a smaller impact on the macroeconomy than an equal change in government spending.

The **tax multiplier** is always one less than the corresponding government spending multiplier because of the lag effect of tax changes showing up as changes in aggregate spending. If we thought of the circular flow model, a tax change has a diversion or leakage into savings prior to the change aggregate spending, whereas a change in government spending changes aggregate spending prior to the initial diversion into savings.

The tax multiplier is found by the formula:

$$MPC \times \frac{1}{MPS}$$

and always assumes a value one less than the multiplier.

In the example cited above, the ultimate impact on the macroeconomy of a $1 increase in taxes would be a $9 decrease in equilibrium national income, as shown below.

$$.9 \times (1/.1) = .9 \times 10 = 9$$

Key 43 Balanced budget multiplier

OVERVIEW *The balanced budget multiplier is a hypothesis that states that if government spending and taxes are increased or decreased simultaneously by equal amounts, GDP will be increased or decreased by the same amount.*

The **balanced budget multiplier** is exactly one; that is, an increase in government purchases, accompanied by an equal increase in taxes, increases the level of income by exactly the amount of the increase in purchases. The reason for that is that the effects of equal increases in government spending and taxes are opposite.

Example: An equal increase in government spending and taxes of $10 billion will raise GDP by $10 billion × 1 = $10 billion.

Note, however, that a balanced budget cut in government purchases has a stronger impact on **equilibrium income** than a dollar cut in taxes. A dollar cut in taxes leads only to a fraction of a dollar's increase in consumption spending, the rest being saved, while government purchases are reflected dollar-for-dollar in a change in aggregate demand.

Key 44 Fiscal policy

OVERVIEW *Fiscal policy is the overall program for directing government spending and taxation for the purpose of keeping the actual GDP close to the potential full employment GDP, but without overreaching that potential and causing inflation.*

Fiscal policy endeavors to avoid excessive unemployment and idle production capability and to create conditions whereby the economy can achieve a growth rate that is neither too rapid nor too slow.

The prescriptions of fiscal policy are straightforward. To counter recessionary conditions in the economy, the federal government should, through fiscal policy, seek to generate a budget deficit by either increasing government spending or decreasing taxes or a combination of both.

When the economy is plagued with excessive unemployment, low levels of output, and overall recessionary conditions, then there is a need to pump dollars and purchasing power into the economy so as to increase spending levels.

In recession, the problem tends to be a level of aggregate demand (or total spending) too low to permit production to reach full employment. There is unused capacity and there are unemployed workers. Thus, the overall demand for goods and services needs to be increased.

One way to accomplish this is for the federal government to lower taxes so that the private sector will have extra dollars to spend for goods and services. When taxes are lowered so that the private sector will have more dollars to spend, then the effect is to increase purchasing power in the **private sector** of the economy.

An alternative is to boost aggregate demand by raising the levels of government spending for public purposes. In either case, aggregate demand should be stimulated; however, it does make a difference which method is used.

Both lower taxes and higher government spending will generate a multiplier effect. Hence, whenever there is a general need to stimulate spending and purchasing power, the amount of the stimulus that is needed is something less than the entire amount of the gap between the actual GDP and the potential GDP.

Example: If the gap between the actual GDP and the potential GDP is $50 billion and if the multiplier is five (because the economy-wide MPC equals .8), then it will be sufficient for the federal government to stimulate the economy with only a $10 billion change in spending (either by a tax reduction or a spending increase), letting the multiplier effect to do the rest.

Key 45 Inflationary effects

OVERVIEW *Inflation causes problems mainly when the rate of price increase changes unexpectedly, and when the inflation rate is so high people will not accept dollars in trade. Inflation affects different people differently.*

Inflation is a reduction in the purchasing power of income and wealth of many people.

The effects of inflation are not distributed equally. Most people suffer from it, but others sometime benefit. Wealth is redistributed between debtors and creditors. For example, debtors benefit in times of inflation.

The **redistribution** is not on the basis of income levels, number of dependents, or other socially acceptable economic criteria.

It also impairs a nation's efficiency and growth.

Governments such as the U.S. that rely on progressive income taxes are major beneficiaries of inflation. The proportion of income collected increases as taxes increase.

Inflation can:
- Cause a reduction in the output of goods and services.
- Reduce the incentive to save.
- Cause uncertainty over future price levels and interest rates and therefore decrease long-term investment in plants and equipment.

Key 46 Budget deficits

OVERVIEW *A budget deficit is created when total expenditures exceed total revenues.*

The **budget surplus** (or **deficit**) in a particular year depends not only on the level of expenditure and the rates set for various taxes and transfers, but also on the rate of GDP during the year.

To get a better measure of changes in discretionary fiscal policy, economists supplement knowledge of the budget by separating the actual budget into its structural and cyclical components.

  1. The **structural budget** calculates how much the government would collect and spend if the economy were operating at full potential output.
  2. The **cyclical budget** calculates the impact of the business cycle on tax revenues, expenditures, and the deficit.

For measuring the impact of fiscal policy on the economy, we should pay close attention to the **structural deficit**; changes in the **cyclical deficit** are a result of changes in the economy rather than a cause of changes in the economy.

The other important factor in weighing the proper deficit is the desired **fiscal monetary mix.** A high investment strategy calls for running a budget surplus along with an expansionary monetary policy. The mix in practice has evolved toward very loose fiscal and tight monetary policy—a sure recipe for a low ratio of investment to GDP and for slow growth of potential output.

Deficits tend to "crowd out" investments. This statement only makes sense for structural deficits (i.e., for policies that raise the structural deficit).

The **public debt** does not burden the shoulders of a nation as if its citizens were forced to carry rocks on their backs. To the degree that we borrow from abroad for consumption and pledge posterity to pay back the interest and principal on such external debt, we do place upon that posterity a net burden. This will mortgage the future generation.

In addition, there may be a serious cost if the public debt displaces capital in people's portfolios. This arises because firms' bonds and common stocks are good substitutes for government bonds. Hence, an increase in government debt may reduce the economy's capital stock.

It is important, also, to keep in perspective the size of the **federal debt** in relation to gross national product and interest charges. The growth of the debt must be appraised in terms of the growth of the economy as a whole. From 1945 to 1980, the ratio of government debt to private debt and to gross national product fell substantially, but the ratio of debt to GDP had risen sharply during the 1980s.

Key 47 Automatic stabilizers

OVERVIEW *Automatic stabilizers, or built-in stabilizers, are automatic corrective devices that reduce the violent price and income swings of the business cycle. Most stabilizers are fiscal in nature.*

Automatic stabilizers are elements in the economy that support aggregate demand when it would otherwise be weak (e.g., during a recession), and hold down aggregate demand when it would otherwise be increasing (e.g., during an expansionary period). This allows the economy to reduce the sensitivity of shifts in demand.

Examples are:
- Income taxes.
- Corporate profits tax.
- Unemployment insurance.
- Farm aid programs.

The most important are **personal** and **corporate income taxes**, which rise and fall with personal and business income and serve both to slow down too rapid expansion (through higher taxes) and to stimulate a sagging economy (through lower taxes).

Unemployment compensation (and similar forms of transfer payment), which counteract slowdowns by affording payments to the jobless; and farm aid programs, which cushion the sometimes wild fluctuations in farm prices, are two other examples.

Paul Samuelson (*Economics,* 10th ed. McGraw-Hill, 1986) pointed out that corporate savings (reflected in continuity of dividend payments to shareholders despite short-term changes in corporate income) and family savings (continued propensity to save even if income rises) similarly act as built-in stabilizers.

Key 48 Full-employment budget

OVERVIEW *Economists have resolved the problem of trying to determine whether the government's fiscal policy was contractionary or expansionary via the concept of a full employment budget.*

The **full employment budget** indicates what the federal budgetary surplus or deficit would be if the economy operated at full employment conditions throughout the year.

Or, to put it another way, the full employment budget (surplus or deficit) measures what the budget position of the federal government would be if the economy were operating at full employment and the prevailing legislative tax and spending programs were in effect.

If the full employment budget is in a surplus position when the economy is operating below full employment, then fiscal policy would actually be restrictive even though the actual budget might be in deficit with the economy operating below full employment conditions. It would be proper to conclude that fiscal policy programs were, in actuality, expansionary.

Theme 7 MONEY, FINANCIAL MARKETS, AND THE BANKING SYSTEM

*M*oney is used to buy goods or services. Money includes cash, checking accounts, and savings accounts. The Federal Reserve Bank helps to control the money supply and formulates monetary policy.

There are three types of demands for money: Transaction, precautionary, and speculative. Commercial banks make loans with the deposits they receive. They are unique in that their loans increase demand deposits and, hence, the money supply. Money markets are short-term credit markets for debt instruments such as commercial paper, certificates of deposit, and treasury bills.

Capital markets are for long-term securities issued by companies and government such as bonds and stock.

Key 49 Meaning and function of money

OVERVIEW *The most important characteristic of money is that we can use it directly to pay for things we buy.*

The assets in our economy that most closely fit this definition are **cash** and **checking accounts. Savings accounts** are good substitutes for checking accounts because you can get use of the saving deposit very quickly, even though you cannot actually make a payment by handing someone your savings passbook. Sometimes we use broader definitions of money that include time and savings deposits.

The official definitions of money have been expanded to include many different assets (Key 29).

Money has traditionally been defined by four functions:
1. **Medium of exchange.**
2. **Store of value.**
3. **Unit of account.**
4. **Standard of deferred payment.**

Key 50 Financial instruments

OVERVIEW *A financial instrument is a document issued by a business or government in exchange for funds (money saving) from savers and traded in financial markets composed of money markets and capital markets.*

Money markets (credit markets) are markets that trade short-term (less than one year) debt instruments. Equity instruments, such as common stock, are traded in the capital market.

A **debt financial instrument** is a contract between the borrower and lender that specifies the amount the borrower must repay, the interest to be paid on the sum borrowed, and the maturity of the obligation. It is also called a **bond.**

While also involving the transfer of funds, an equity financial instrument does not contractually require repayment of the amount borrowed nor require a specific interest payment. Rather, the saver receives a financial instrument that specifies partial ownership and control of the firm and a promise of sharing in the firm's profits. It is also called a **share of stock.**

Examples of money market securities include:
- U.S. Treasury bills.
- Federal agency securities.
- Bankers' acceptances.
- Commercial paper.
- Negotiable certificates of deposit issued by government, business, and financial institutions.

The **money market instruments** are characterized by their highly liquid nature and a relatively low default risk.

Certificates of deposit (CDs) are issued by commercial banks and thrift institutions and have traditionally been in amounts of $10,000 or $100,000 (jumbo CDs). CDs have a fixed maturity period varying from several months to many years.

Commercial paper is issued by large corporations on a discount basis to the public. It usually comes in minimum denominations of $25,000 and represents an unsecured promissory note of financially strong companies. It usually carries a higher yield than small CDs. The maturity is generally thirty, sixty, and ninety days.

Treasury bills have a maximum maturity of one year and common maturities of 91 and 182 days. They trade in minimum units of $10,000. They do not pay interest in the traditional sense; they are sold at a discount, and redeemed when the maturity date comes around at face value. T-bills have an extremely low risk because they are backed by the U.S. government.

Repurchase agreements (repos) are a form of loan in which the borrower sells securities (such as government securities and other marketable securities) to the lender, but simultaneously contracts to repurchase the same securities either on call or on a specified date at a price that will produce an agreed yield.

Bankers' acceptances (BAs) are drafts drawn on a bank by a corporation to pay for merchandise. The draft promises payment of a certain sum of money to its holder at some future date. What makes BAs unique is that by prearrangement a bank accepts them, thereby guaranteeing their payment at the stated time. Most BAs arise in foreign trade transactions. It is a marketable instrument. The most common maturity for BAs is three months, although they can have maturities of up to 270 days. Their typical denominations are $500,000 and $1 million.

Capital market instruments are long-term securities issued by the government and corporations.

They cover both **debt-instruments (bonds)** and **equities (common and preferred stocks).**

Relative to money market instruments, those of the capital market often carry greater default and market risks but return a relatively high yield in compensation for the higher risks.

Key 51 Financial institutions and
markets

OVERVIEW *A healthy economy depends heavily on efficient transfer of funds from savers to individuals, businesses, and governments. Most transfers occur through specialized financial institutions that serve as intermediaries between suppliers and users of funds.*

Financial intermediaries are firms that serve as middlemen between lenders and borrowers. In general, they are wholesalers and retailers of funds. Examples of such firms are:
- Commercial banks.
- Mutual savings banks.
- Savings and loan associations.
- Insurance companies.
- Credit unions.

Financial markets provide a mechanism through which the financial manager may obtain funds from a wide range of sources, including financial institutions.

In the financial markets, entities demanding funds are brought together with those having surplus funds.

The financial markets are composed of **money markets** and **capital markets:**
1. **Money markets** (credit markets) are the markets for short-term (less than one year) debt securities.
    - Equity instruments such as common stock are not traded in the money market.
    - Examples of money market securities include U.S. Treasury bills, federal agency securities, bankers' acceptances, commercial paper, and negotiable certificates of deposit issued by government, business, and financial institutions.
    - Money market securities are characterized by their highly liquid nature and have a relatively low default risk.
2. **Capital markets** are markets in which long-term securities issued by the government and corporations are traded.
    - Unlike the money market, both debt-instruments (bonds) and equities (common and preferred stocks) are traded.

- Relative to money market instruments, those of the capital market often carry greater default and market risks but return a relatively high yield in compensation for the higher risks.
- The New York Stock Exchange, which handles the stock of many of the larger corporations, is a prime example of a capital market. The American Stock Exchange and the regional stock exchanges are still other examples. These exchanges are organized markets.

Securities are also traded through the thousands of brokers and dealers on the over-the-counter (or unlisted) market, a term used to denote an informal system of contacts among brokers and dealers. Most corporate bonds are traded over-the-counter.

A **primary market** refers to the market for new issues, while a **secondary market** is where previously issued, "secondhand" securities are exchanged. The New York Stock Exchange is an example of a secondary market.

There are other markets that trade special types of financial instruments.
- The **commodity markets** handle various commodity futures.
- The **foreign exchange market** involves international financial transactions between the U.S. and other countries.
- The **mortgage market** handles real estate financing and mortgage-backed securities.

Key 52 Federal Reserve System

OVERVIEW *The Federal Reserve System is the system, created by an act of Congress in 1913, that is made up of twelve Federal Reserve District Banks, their twenty-five branches, and all national and state banks (about 5,700 member banks) that are part of the system scattered throughout the nation. It is headed by a seven-member Board of Governors (Figure 1).*

The main structure of the **Federal Reserve System** consists of twelve Federal Reserve banks, twenty-five branches of these banks, the Board of Governors, the Federal Open Market Committee, and the member banks.

The **Federal Reserve banks** are owned by member banks, which are required to subscribe to Federal Reserve stock in an amount equal to 6 percent (in practice, only 3 percent has been required) of their paid-in capital and surplus. Annual dividends to stockholders cannot exceed 6 percent of the paid-in capital. Recently, any Fed earnings in excess of dividends have been paid to the Treasury. Each Federal Reserve bank has a nine-member board of directors, members of which are selected by the member banks and by the Board of Governors.

The **Board of Governors** consists of seven members, each appointed by the President of the United States with the advice and consent of the Senate. The members serve staggered fourteen-year terms, with one term ending every two years. The President designates one member as chairman and one as vice-chairman. The chairman's term is four years, but it does not run concurrently with the President's.

The Board of Governors has the power to supervise the operations of the Federal Reserve Banks. Within statutory limits it can:
- Determine the types of loans Federal Reserve banks and depository institutions can make.
- Set the reserve requirements for commercial banks and other depository institutions.
- Regulate loans on securities.
- Approve or disapprove discount rates established by the Federal Reserve banks.

The Board of Governors also constitutes a majority of the Federal Open Market Committee.

The **Federal Open Market Committee (FOMC)** determines the amounts of government securities and other obligations that Federal Reserve banks buy or sell and controls Federal Reserve purchases of foreign currencies in the international money markets.

The FOMC has twelve members, seven from the Board of Governors. The other five must either be a president or a vice-president of one of the Federal Reserve banks. One of these five must be from the Federal Reserve Bank of New York; one is from the Federal Reserve banks of Boston, Philadelphia, and Richmond; one is from the Reserve banks of Atlanta, Dallas, and St. Louis; one is from the Reserve banks of Minneapolis, Kansas City, and San Francisco; and one is from the Reserve banks of Cleveland and Chicago. The FOMC meets at least once every three weeks to determine the goals of its open market policy and to prescribe in a general way the actions to be taken. Purchases are carried out by a vice-president of the Reserve Bank of New York.

The **Federal Advisory Council** consists of one representative from each of the twelve Federal Reserve districts. They are selected by the board of directors of the Reserve banks in the respective districts. The Council has no power to ensure that its advice is followed.

To become a member of the Federal Reserve System, a bank must meet certain capital requirements and agree to abide by all of the rules and regulations of the System.

Before 1981, a member bank could use Fed clearing and wire transfer facilities, obtain short-term loans from its Federal Reserve bank, obtain currency as needed, and take advantage of the information services provided by the system. Many of these services were provided free of charge.

However, nonmember banks could also obtain many of these services through correspondent banking relationships without meeting the other requirements of membership.

The **Monetary Control Act of 1980** provided for a uniform reserve requirement for all banks and other depository institutions, and it further required that the Fed charge all depository institutions alike for its services (Keys 53 and 65).

KEY FIGURE 1
Organization and Map of the Federal Reserve System

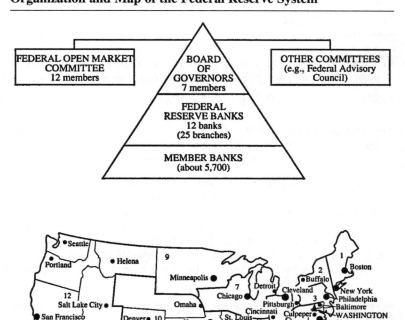

Key 53 Functions of the Federal Reserve

OVERVIEW *The Federal Reserve System, headed by a seven-member Board of Governors, determines the nation's monetary policy, among other things.*

The primary function of the Board is to establish and conduct the nation's monetary policy. The System manages the nation's monetary policy by exercising control over the money stock (Figure 1).

It controls the money supply primarily in three ways:
1. By raising or lowering the reserve requirement.
2. By setting the discount rate for loans to commercial banks.
3. By purchasing and selling the government securities, mainly three-month bills and notes issued by the U.S. Treasury.

The System also serves as the central bank of the United States, offering banks many of the same services that banks provide their customers.

KEY FIGURE 1
Flow of Federal Reserve Influence

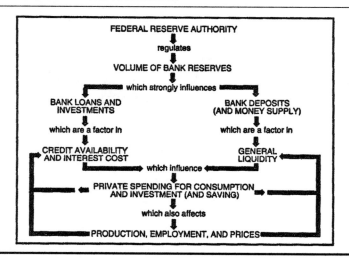

Key 54 Organization of the banking system

OVERVIEW *The history of the United States in establishing a stable monetary and banking system is filled with trial, error, and conflict.*

The **First Bank of the United States** was given a twenty-year charter by the federal government in 1791. The bank's capital stock was owned both by the federal government and private sources.

The First Bank performed all the usual functions of an ordinary commercial bank during its brief history; in addition, it served as a depository for federal government funds, loaned money to the government, transferred government funds, and regulated lending and the issuing of bank notes by state banks.

The charter of the First Bank was not renewed because of concern over the power of the federal government and the effect of the First Bank on state banks, concern about currency in general, and concern that a significant part of the First Bank's stock was owned by foreigners.

The **Second Bank of the United States** received a twenty-year charter from the federal government in 1816. Its capital stock was also owned by the federal government, by private individuals and groups, and by the states.

Similar to the First Bank, the Second Bank performed both central and commercial banking functions. In 1836, the charter of the Second Bank was not renewed for many of the same reasons that the First Bank was disbanded.

In addition, Andrew Jackson, who was president at the time, thought that the Second Bank had become too powerful. His campaign against the Bank and its president, Nicholas Biddle, contributed greatly to the Bank's demise.

The **National Banking Act of 1864** established a system through which private banks could receive a charter from the federal government. However, no further attempts at establishing a central bank were made until the Federal Reserve System was established.

Before the Federal Reserve System was established, the banking system was criticized for not having a centralized banking system that could provide "elasticity" to the money supply. The Fed could control the quantity of money in circulation.

During periods when bank customers became anxious and desired to hold more cash, there was no way to ensure an orderly increase of the quantity of hard currency or paper money in the economy. As a result, serious bank panics occurred in 1873, 1884, 1893, and 1907. Under such circumstances many banks stopped payments and frantically called in loans, and some went out of business.

Moreover, during boom times there was no way to reduce the money supply to limit inflation and overexpansion.

As a result, on December 23, 1913, the **Glass-Owen Bill** (the Federal Reserve Act) was passed. This Act established the Federal Reserve System, which was authorized to control the quantity of money in circulation.

Key 55 How banks create money

OVERVIEW *Commercial banks accept deposits and make loans. They are unique because their loans increase demand deposits and the money supply.*

If banks kept 100 percent cash reserves against all deposits, there would be no multiple creation of money when new, high-powered reserves were injected by the central bank into the system. There would be only a one-to-one exchange of one kind of money for another kind of money.

Modern banks are required by the Federal Reserve to keep legal reserves on their demand deposits, depending on the size of deposits.

While no bank alone can expand its reserves ten to one, the banking system as a whole can. Assume the first individual bank receives a new $1000. If we follow through the successive group of banks in the dwindling, never-ending chain, we find, for the system as a whole, new deposits of

$$\$1000 + \$900 + \$810 + \$729 + \ldots = \$1000 \times 1 + (9/10) + (9/10)^2 + \ldots$$
$$= \$1000(1/(1-9/10)$$
$$= \$1000(1/0.1)$$
$$= \$10,000$$

The potential increase in demand deposits for the commercial banking system is specified as:

$$\Delta D = \Delta R \, (1/r)$$

where ΔD = the potential change in demand deposit volume, r = the reserve requirement, and ΔR = the change in reserve for the banking system. $1/r$ is called the **Demand Deposit Multiplier.**

Example: Assume $r = .1$ and there is a $1,000 increase in actual reserves; that is, $\Delta R = \$1,000$, and $1/r = 1/.1 = 10$.

$$\Delta D = \$1,000 \, (10) = \$10,000$$

The banking system could experience a $10,000 increase in demand deposits.

Key 56 Demand for money balances

OVERVIEW *Money is demanded because of its transactions use and its quality for a store of value.*

Money demand can be of three types:
1. The **transaction demand** for money refers to the demand of households and businesses to hold money balances rather than bonds, stocks, or other financial instruments, in order to carry on everyday purchases and payments. This does not depend on the rate of interest but varies directly with the level of national income only.
2. The **precautionary demand** for money refers to the demand for money to make any unforeseen payments. This, too, depends only on the level of national income.
3. The **speculative demand** for money refers to demand for money in the expectation of higher interest rates in the future; that is, people hold larger money balances if they expect interest rates to rise in the future, rather than tying this money up in bonds now. This speculative demand for money is inversely related to the interest rate. As a result, the *total* demand curve demand for *money* or liquidity is also downward sloped when plotted against interest rates.

Key 57 Federal Reserve and the
money supply

OVERVIEW *The total money supply is regulated largely by the central bank, that is, the Federal Reserve System, but the actual process of money creation takes place in commercial banks.*

The Fed controls money supply through a **monetary policy.** Changes in the money supply, in turn, affect the interest rate—the cost of borrowing—which influence consumers' and businesses' decisions to spend and/or invest.

These decisions affect the levels of output, employment, income, and prices.

There are two basic kinds of monetary policy:
1. An **easy-money policy** expands commercial bank reserves and consequently the economy's money supply. It encourages investment spending because more money means lower interest rates and a greater demand for loans.
2. A **tight-money policy** lowers reserves and reduces the money supply. It discourages investment spending.

Other principal mechanisms whereby the Fed tightens or eases credit— that is, the total money supply—are by changing the discount rate, and engaging in open-market operations.

In addition, the Federal Reserve can exert selective credit controls specifically limiting consumer credit or stock market credit without changing requirements for other kinds of credit, and also through moral suasion.

Raising or lowering the discount rate (the interest rate charged by the Fed to commercial banks borrowing from them) affects how much commercial banks can afford to borrow, and hence how much they can lend.

The Fed can, by buying and selling government securities on the open market, raise or lower commercial banks' reserves, and, thus, their lending ability.

Key 58 Interest and interest rates

OVERVIEW *Interest is the price paid for the use of money or loanable funds, expressed as a percentage of the amount borrowed.*

If the rate of interest is 8 percent per year, this means that for $100 borrowed today, $108 will have to be repaid a year from today. Loanable funds is the total amount of money available for borrowing.

The function of the rate of interest, like the price of other resources, is to allocate the scarce supply of loanable funds to the most productive uses (i.e., to those uses where the net productivity or rate of return on investment are greatest).

This is accomplished because firms borrow and invest as long as the rate of return on investments exceeds the interest rate and up to the level at which they are equal. However, the government directly allocates some public investments to highways, schools, hospitals and other public projects without regard to their profitability.

In addition, the greater bargaining power of larger firms may allow them to borrow at lower rates than smaller firms and thus enter into some investments that are less productive than those that could be made by smaller firms.

The **equilibrium interest rate** is determined at the intersection of the market demand and supply curves of loanable funds.

The **demand for loanable funds** comes from the borrowing of firms, consumers and government, and is negatively sloped. To maximize profits, a firm will borrow to invest in machinery, inventory, and the like, as long as the return, or marginal productivity, of the investment exceeds the rate of interest on borrowed funds. Thus, interest rates allocate the scarce Loanable Funds to the most productive uses.

The **supply of loanable funds** stems from the past and current savings of individuals and firms. It is upward sloped, and is greatly affected by monetary policy.

In the real world, we do not have a single rate of interest but a whole structure of many different rates of interest. Each of these rates depend on the risk, maturity, administrative cost of the loan, and on the competitiveness of the loanable-fund market.

In general, the interest rate on a loan is higher and as such:
- The greater the risk of borrower default.
- The longer the term of the loan.
- The smaller the amount of the loan (i.e. administering many small loans costs much more than administering one larger loan, everything else remaining the same).
- The less competitive the financial system (i.e. a single financial institution in an isolated locality can charge higher interest rates on loans than if there were several such lenders).

When we speak of the rate of interest, we usually refer to the pure rate of interest. This is the rate of interest on riskless loans and is roughly equal to the interest rate on long-term government bonds that will almost certainly be repaid.

Other interest rates are higher and depend on the four factors listed above. Generally, when the pure rate of interest rises, the whole structure of interest rates also rises.

TYPES OF INTEREST RATES:
Broad trends are detected by focusing on two rates. One is the **prime rate,** which is what banks charge their best customers for short-term loans. When the prime rate is climbing, it means companies are borrowing heavily and the economy is still on an upward swing. The second rate you should follow is the yield on **90-day Treasury bills.** When yields on 90-day bills rise sharply, this may signal a resurgence of inflation. Subsequently, the economy could slow down. Interest rates are controlled by the Fed's monetary policy. The Fed's monetary policy tools involve: (1) changes in the required reserve ratio; (2) changes in the discount rate; and (3) open market operations—that is, purchase and sale of government securities. The **discount rate** is the interest rate the Fed charges its member banks to "cover their requirement." If the bank's reserves fall below the required level, the bank can borrow reserves from the Fed—for a price. Raise the discount rate, and banks will be loathe to loan up to their limit. More important, most institutional lenders index their loan rates to the Fed's discount rate. Therefore, an increase in the discount rate will send all interest rates up.

Cuts in the discount rate are aimed at stimulating the economy—a positive development for stocks. The discussion below summarizes the effect of cutting the discount rate on the economy.

THE EFFECTS OF LOWERING THE DISCOUNT RATE:
- **The players.** The Federal Reserve is the nation's central bank. It regulates the flow of money through the economy.

- **The action.** Discount rate is what the Federal Reserve charges on short-terms loans to member banks. When the Fed cuts the discount rate, it means banks can get cash cheaper and thus charge less on loans.
- **The first effect.** Within a few days, banks are likely to start passing on the discounts by cutting their prime rate, which is what banks charge on loans to their best corporate customers.
- **Impact.** Businesses are more likely to borrow. Also, adjustable consumer loans are tied to the prime, such as credit card rates. These become cheaper, stimulating spending.
- **The second effect.** Within a few weeks, rates on mortgage and auto and construction loans drop.
- **The third effect.** The lower rates go, the more investors move their cash to stocks, creating new wealth.
- **The goal.** To kick-start the economy. If lower interest rates cause businesses to start growing again, laid-off workers get jobs, retailers start selling, and the economy starts to roll again.

Some other important interest rates are briefly explained below.

1. **Federal funds rate.** This is the rate on short-term loans among commercial banks for overnight use. The Fed influences this rate by open market operations and by changing the bank's required reserve.
2. **Discount rate.** This is the charge on loans to depository institutions by the Fed. A change in the discount rate is considered a major economic event and is expected to have an impact on security prices, especially bonds. A change in the prime rate usually follows the change in the discount rate.
3. **5-year Treasury notes.** The yields on these notes give you an idea of the prevailing interest rates for intermediate-term fixed-income securities.
4. **10-year Treasury bonds.** This yield, also called the **long bond yield,** is a closely watched indicator of long-term interest rates since the entire bond market (and sometimes the stock market as well) often moves in line with this rate.

Note: The Wall Street Journal carries key interest rates. Federal Reserve Bank of St. Louis charts these key rates and others.

Theme 8 MONETARY POLICY

E quilibrium income occurs when there is an equality between planned saving and planned investment. When investment spending is specified as a function of the rate of interest, equilibrium income depends on the rate of interest.

The marginal efficiency of investment relates to the range of projects available to a company based on their return rates. Under the quantity theory of money, spending and prices are directly proportional to the money in circulation. The money supply is determined by the Fed's creation of money, and the reserve requirement on deposit balances.

Monetary policy is based on the overall supply of money, available credit, and interest rates.

Key 59 Price level and inflation

OVERVIEW *Inflation means that prices in general are on the rise, not necessarily that all prices rise by the same amount. Some prices may not rise at all, and some may even fall.*

In addition:
- Some prices tend to change rather rapidly and smoothly, reflecting changes in market forces, such as the quantity and velocity of money.
- The prices of agricultural products such as beef and wheat tend to mirror changes in their auction markets with reasonable rapidity.
- The prices of many other goods take time to adjust upward. Price increases may be delayed when long time lags exist between the placement of an order and the delivery of the product, or when contracts specify the price at the time of delivery.
- If the prices of products rise at different rates, then wages are likely to follow at different rates. Hence, not all reductions in the purchasing power of income can be attributed to inflation.

Key 60 Income and interest rates

OVERVIEW *In the two-sector model, equilibrium income occurs where planned saving (S) equals planned investment, i.e., S = I, or equivalently, where aggregate output equals planned spending. When investment spending is specified as a function of the rate of interest, equilibrium income depends on the rate of interest.*

When investment spending is negatively related to the interest rate, equilibrium income varies inversely with the rate of interest, i.e., $Y = Y(i)$.

Equilibrium income consistent with selected interest rates is plotted in Figure 1 with the schedule labeled *IS*.

The *IS* schedule shows the combinations of Y and i at which there is equality between planned saving (S) and planned investment (I).

When the saving (or consumption) function and the investment function are specified, an equation for the IS schedule can be derived and the equilibrium level of income that is consistent with various rates of interest can be determined.

Example: Suppose $S = -\$50 + 0.10Y$ and $I = \$200 - 5i$. Equilibrium occurs where

$$S = I$$
$$-\$50 + 0.10Y = \$200 - 5i$$
$$0.10Y = \$250 - 5i$$
$$Y = \$2,500 - 50i$$

When the rate of interest is 6 percent, $Y = \$2,500 - 50(6) = \$2,200$.

KEY FIGURE 1

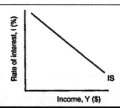

Key 61 Investment and interest rates

OVERVIEW *Firms sell securities to raise the funds to finance their investment spending. Each firm has a list of projects ranging from those yielding a high rate of return to those yielding a low rate of return. This list is shown by the marginal efficiency of investment curve.*

Marginal Efficiency of Investment (MEI) is the expected annual percentage rate of return on additional investment spending.

MEI is determined by such factors as:

- The stock of capital available to meet market demands.
- Technology and innovation.
- The demand for the product to be produced by the investment.

An MEI curve (Figure 1) is a demand curve for investment showing the relationship between real interest rates and investment spending. It shows also the amount of investment spending that firms are willing to undertake at each rate of interest (or cost of capital).

KEY FIGURE 1

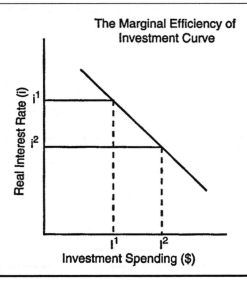

The Marginal Efficiency of Investment Curve

Key 62 Quantity theory of money

OVERVIEW *The quantity theory of money is the idea that the level of spending and prices is directly proportional to the amount of money in circulation, so that an increase in circulating money will raise prices and a decrease will lower prices.*

Stated as early as the 17th century (by Hume, among others), this theory was generally accepted by economists, from the classical school through Alfred Marshall.

In its simple form, it assumes that prices always are proportional to the total money supply. (Marshall devised an equation, expressing this relationship: $N = Y/K$, where N is the total number of monetary units, Y is the level of money income, and K is the sum of consumer goods and services.)

However, neither basic assumption is valid. Sometimes more efficient production increases the total output and prices need not rise much (or at all) for the producer to increase profits; in that case prices clearly are not proportional to total spending.

Further, the total money supply is not a simple constant, and total spending represents a flow of income over time; the quantity theory fails to take into account the rate of that flow (the so-called velocity of circulation of money). Nevertheless, variations of the theory, popularized in the United States by Irving Fisher, continue to be propounded by some economists, notably Milton Friedman.

The **equation of exchange** is a mathematical expression of the **quantity theory of money** devised by Irving Fisher.

It is basically a statement of the fundamental principle that the aggregate amount spent by buyers is equal to the total value of the goods and services sold.

Mathematically, the equation is an identity, expressed as follows:

$$MV = PQ$$

where M = money supply, V = income velocity of money, P = average price of final goods and services produced during the year, and Q = physical quantity of those goods and services.

Example: If the supply of money is $300 billion and each of these dollars on the average is spent five times a year for currently produced goods and services, total expenditures for currently produced goods and services will be $1,500 billion. If producers turn out 750 billion "units" of goods and services and these are subsequently sold at an average price of $2 per unit, then the value of these currently produced goods and services, or GDP, is $1,500 billion. In other words,

$$MV = PQ$$
$$(\$300 \text{ billion})(5) = (\$2)(750 \text{ billion units})$$
$$\$1{,}500 \text{ billion} = \$1{,}500 \text{ billion}$$

The equation of exchange is very important because it provides insights into what will happen to output (Q) and prices (P) when the money supply (M) changes.

Example: Assume that the velocity of money (V) is constant. If M increases, then either P or Q or both must increase. The effects of P and Q will depend on the state of the economy.
1. If the economy is operating well below the full employment level, Q will tend to rise relatively more than P as unemployed resources are re-employed.
2. If the economy is at full employment, P will tend to rise more than Q, i.e., the increase in M will be purely inflationary.

Key 63 Interest and money demand

OVERVIEW *The reasons for holding money balances include a transaction, a precautionary, and a portfolio demand for money.*

The **transaction demand for money** refers to the demand of households and businesses to hold money balances in order to carry on their everyday purchases and payments. This does not depend on the rate of interest but varies directly with the level of national income only.

The **precautionary demand for money** refers to the demand for money in order to make any unforeseen payments. This, too, depends only on the level of national income.

The **portfolio demand for money** refers to demand for money in the expectation of higher interest rates; that is, people hold larger money balances if they expect interest rates to rise in the future, rather than tying this money up in bonds now. This demand for money is inversely related to the interest rate.

As a result, the total demand curve for money or liquidity is downward sloped when plotted against interest rates (See Figure 1).

KEY FIGURE 1

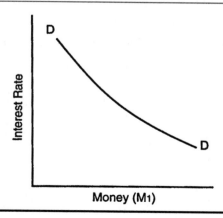

Money (M1)

Key 64 Supply of and demand for

money

OVERVIEW *There are factors that determine the supply of and demand for money. The money supply (M1) is determined by the Fed's creation of money, the reserve requirement on deposit balances and the like.*

The M1 money supply is the product of the monetary base B and money multiplier, or

$$M1 = m1\ B$$

m1 is the *money multiplier* and equals

$$\frac{(1 + k)}{(k + r + t\ rT + e)}$$

where k = the currency ratio (the ratio of currency preferences relative to checking deposits), r = the reserve requirement, t = the ratio of large time deposits to checking deposits, rT = the reserve requirement on large time deposits, and e = the excess reserve ratio (the quantity of excess reserve held by depository institutions relative to checking deposits).

Example: Suppose monetary base $B = \$400{,}000$, $r = .1$, $rT = .05$, $k = .2$, $t = 1$, and $e = .05$. The *m1* money multiplier is

$$(1 + .2)/(.2 + .1 + 1\ (.05) + .05) = 3$$

Then the M1 money supply is $\$400{,}000 \times 3 = \$1{,}200{,}000$

Key 65 Tools of monetary policy

OVERVIEW *Monetary policy is a deliberate exercise of the Federal Reserve's power to induce changes in the money supply in order to achieve price stability, to help smooth out business cycles, and to bring the economy's employment and output to desired levels.*

Monetary policy is essentially directed at regulating the economy's overall money supply, credit availability, and, to a lesser degree, the level of interest rates by the Federal Reserve System.

The Federal Reserve System has three major devices that it can use to control the money supply:
1. Changes in the required reserve ratio.
2. Changes in the discount rate.
3. Open market operations, that is, purchase and sale of government securities.

Minor tools include the margin requirement on securities, other selective credit controls, and moral suasion.

Reserve requirements. The Board of Governors is responsible for determining the reserve requirements of depository institutions within broad limits set by Congress.

Open market operations. Open market operations consist of buying and selling securities on the open market. The term "open market" refers to the market for highly liquid, predominantly short-term securities, especially securities of the United States government. This is the method used most frequently by the Fed to adjust the money supply.

The **discount rate.** The discount rate is the interest rate that a Federal Reserve Bank charges a depository institution when it gives the institution a loan. The Fed expects financial institutions to request loans only under special circumstances. As a result, although changes in the discount rate have "announcement effects" played up in the news media, they are not a very important monetary policy tool.

Margin requirements on securities. The margin requirement is the percent of the current market price of securities that must be used as a down payment. During 1986, the margin requirement was 50 percent.

Moral suasion. Moral suasion occurs when the Federal Reserve attempts to achieve its policy goals by publicly urging banks or the general public to do one thing or another.

Selective Credit Controls.

- **Regulation W** of the Federal Reserve instituted selective consumer credit controls during World War II. It regulated consumer credit for items other than housing by specifying the minimum down payments and the maximum maturity of installment loans and length of time charge accounts could run.
- **Regulation X** placed selective credit controls on financing for new residential construction during the Korean War.
- The **Credit Control Act of 1969** authorizes such actions to be taken on the part of the President. In March of 1980, President Carter placed tighter restrictions on credit card issuers. These rules were suspended in the summer of that year.

Regulation Q. Formerly, the Federal Reserve established the maximum rates that banks and savings and loan associations could pay on their time and saving deposit liabilities through Regulation Q. However, this policy resulted in problems caused by disintermediation, a process whereby individuals and businesses reduce their deposits at commercial banks and other depository institutions in order to invest directly in other assets. The Monetary Control Act provided for the phasing out of Regulation Q by 1986.

Federal funds rate. The Federal funds rate is the rate that commercial banks charge each other when they loan their excess reserves, usually on a one-day basis. The Federal funds rate has increased in importance in recent years as financial institutions have more aggressively tried to maximize profits. Moreover, because there are no prohibitions on borrowing or lending of federal funds, the federal funds rate has a significant effect on bank credit policies.

Theme 9   FULL
MACROECONOMIC
MODEL

*O*verall macroeconomic equilibrium is where the aggregate supply and aggregate demand curves intersect. The curves determine the aggregate price and output. In the short-term, the aggregate supply curve is upward sloping, meaning the increasing prices result in greater GDP and employment. In the long-term, the curve is vertical. As supply increases, prices decrease.

Aggregate demand is the total output demanded at a specified price level over a stated time period. It is the total of consumption, investment, government, and net export expenditures. As prices increase, demand decreases. The relationship between inflation and unemployment is indicated by the Phillips Curve.

The money and goods markets provide the model of macroeconomic activity. These markets are tied together by real output and the interest rate.

Key 66 Aggregate supply and
demand: Equilibrium

OVERVIEW *AS and AD curves have the same shapes as the familiar microeconomic supply and demand curves, although the reasons behind the slopes are different here.*

Aggregate demand slopes down in part because consumers are able to stretch their dollar incomes and wealth further at a lower price level (Key 71).

In the short run (for all but very high output levels), the **AS curve** slopes gently upward, so the level of real output is primarily determined by where the **AD curve** cuts the nearly flat AS curve (Key 67).

In the long run, the AS curve turns vertical. This reflects the fact that in the long run all costs are variable, so the cost structure will follow output prices. Because long-run AS is vertical at potential output, the long-run level of potential output determines that level of output. This result arises from the intersection of a downward-sloping AD curve with a vertical AS curve (Key 68).

The **overall macroeconomic equilibrium,** determining both aggregate price and output, comes where the AS and AD curves intersect (Figures 1 and 2).

KEY FIGURE 1

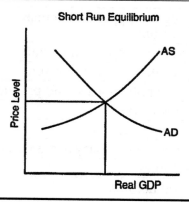

Short Run Equilibrium

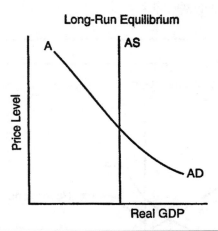

Long-Run Equilibrium

Recent American experience provides important applications of the AS-AD apparatus.

In the mid-1960s, Vietnam war-bloated deficits plus easy money led to a rapid outward shift in the AD curve. The result was a sharp upturn in prices and inflation.

In the early 1970s, a series of adverse "supply shocks" led to an upward movement in the AS curve. This led to a reduction of output along with an increase in prices and inflation.

At the end of the 1970s, economic policy makers induced a sharp recession to reduce inflation. Tight money shifted the AD curve to the left—in effect reversing the measures taken during the Vietnam war. The stagnation of the early 1980s led to a sharp reduction in inflation along with high unemployment.

In the **Keynesian** model, equilibrium can occur below, at, or above the level of real GDP corresponding to full employment of resources.

Potential GDP is the level of real GDP attainable if unemployment equaled 4 percent.

A recessionary or inflationary gap exists when the equilibrium level of real GDP does not coincide with the potential real GDP.

A recessionary gap exists when the equilibrium real GDP is less than the potential real GDP (Figure 3). Recessionary gap = Potential real GDP – Equilibrium real GDP.

KEY FIGURE 3

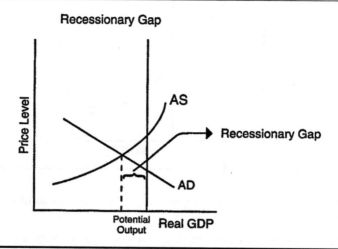

Recessionary Gap

An inflationary gap exists when the equilibrium level of real GDP is greater than the potential real GDP (Figure 4).

KEY FIGURE 4

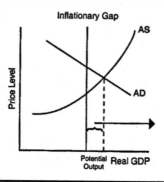

Recessionary gaps are characterized by higher rates of unemployment or underemployment of resources, and slower economic growth than would exist at potential real GDP. The Keynesian theory implies that there will be only minimal upward pressure on prices during such a period, due to competition between underemployed plants and unemployed workers.

Inflationary gaps are characterized by lower unemployment rates, higher utilization of industrial capacity, and a larger backlog of orders among producers than would exist at potential real GDP.

The Keynesian theory implies that there will be upward pressure on prices, and that demand-pull inflation is likely to result.

Key 67 Aggregate supply: Short run

OVERVIEW *The aggregate supply (AS) curve is upward sloping in the short run. This means that rising prices bring forth higher levels of real GDP and employment.*

The **short run** is the period of time when nominal (or dollar) factor costs do not change. In the short run, factor costs (such as wages and machine costs) are often slow to adjust to changing price levels. Costs tend to be "sticky." Wages, for example, are often fixed by long-term contracts and take time to change. In the short run then, a higher price level means more profits for firms, profits that firms pursue by increasing output. So the aggregate supply curve has a positive slope in the short run (Figure 1).

The **AS curve** has a positive slope. It gets steeper as the full employment level of real GDP is approached because, as increasing quantities of the economy's resources are utilized, labor and other resources become scarcer and more expensive.

The AS curve will shift for a change in any one of the *ceteris paribus* variables. Factors that shift the AS curve are those that cause changes in business costs, including wages, raw material costs, business taxes, and government regulations.

The AS curve is a snapshot at one point in time.

KEY FIGURE 1

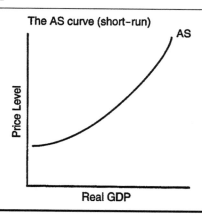

The AS curve (short-run)

Key 68 Aggregate supply: Long run

OVERVIEW *The long-run aggregate supply (AS) curve is vertical. The long run is the period of time over which input costs, such as wages, are free to adjust. Long run (in macroeconomics) refers to the time it takes the economy to come to a complete full-employment equilibrium.*

In the long run:
- All contracts (such as those between employers and workers) can be rewritten so that contracted-for wages reflect the actual price level and so that any false expectations (about price level) that cause unemployment are eliminated.
- Workers will set their wages such that they will be fully employed. Thus, output will be at its full-employment level.
- Output will be at **FE (Full Employment)** no matter what the price level. The long-run AS curve is a vertical line at full employment (Figure 1). This means that the price level can fluctuate with changes in aggregate demand while real GDP remains stable at its full level.
- Price level will be determined by where the aggregate demand curve intersects the long-run aggregate supply curve (Key 66). At this price level, the economy will be at full employment.

The level of unemployment that exists at full employment is called the **natural rate of unemployment.** If unemployment is above its natural rate, wages (and thus costs and prices) tend to fall. And if unemployment is below its natural rate, wages (and thus costs and prices) tend to rise.

KEY FIGURE 1

The AS Curve (Long Run)

Price Level

Real GDP

Key 69 Labor supply, wages, and productivity

OVERVIEW *The wage rate (or money-wage rate) refers to the earnings per hour of labor.*

The **money-wage rate** divided by the price index gives the **real wage rate** or **actual "purchasing power"** of money wages. We are primarily concerned with real wages.

The level of **real wages** depends on the productivity of labor. Real wages are higher; for example,
- the greater the amount of capital available per worker.
- the more advanced the technology of production.
- the greater the availability of a variety of natural resources (i.e., fertile land or mineral deposits).

We saw that firms demand labor (and other resources) in order to produce the products demanded by customers. By adding each firm's demand for labor, we get the **market demand** for labor.

On the other hand, the **market supply** of labor depends on:
- the population size.
- the proportion of the population in the labor force.
- the state of the economy (such as boom or recession).
- the level of real wages.
- the level of technological ability or the educational attainment.

The **competitive equilibrium real-wage rate** is determined at the intersection of the market demand and supply of labor curves. The firm then hires labor until the marginal revenue product of labor (MRP_L) or its demand of labor (d_L) equals the wage rate.

Workers are often not hired competitively. In a company town, a firm is the only or dominant employer with monopoly power in the local labor market and is referred to as a **monopsonist.**

A monopsonist faces the rising market supply curve of labor, which indicates that it must pay higher wages to hire more workers. As a result, the change in the total cost of hiring an additional unit of labor or **Marginal Resource Cost of Labor** (MRC_L) exceeds the wage rate.

To maximize total profits, the firm hires labor until $MRP_L = MRC_L$ and pays the wage indicated on the supply curve of labor for that quantity of labor.

Labor unions attempt to increase wages in three ways:

1. They attempt to increase the demand for labor by increasing labor productivity, by financing advertising of union-made products and by lobbying to restrict imports. This is the most desirable, but also the least effective, method.
2. They attempt to raise wages by restricting the supply of labor through the imposition of high initiation fees and long apprenticeships and requirements that employers hire only union members. This is done primarily by craft unions (i.e. unions of such skilled workers as electricians).
3. They attempt to raise wage rates directly by bargaining with employers, using a variety of tactics, such as slowdowns or calling for a boycott of the firm's products. Strikes today are not as common as they were twenty or more years ago. This method is used primarily by **industrial unions** (i.e. unions of all the workers of a particular industry, such as automobile workers). Empirical studies seem to indicate that in general, unions in the U.S. have raised real wages for their members by only about 10 to 15 percent.

If all jobs and individuals were exactly alike and all markets perfectly competitive, there would be a single wage for all jobs and all workers. However, jobs requiring equal qualifications may differ in attractiveness, and higher wages must be paid to attract and retain workers in more unpleasant jobs.

Such wage differentials are known as **equalizing differences.** Even if all jobs were equally attractive, wage differences would persist because individuals such as doctors, accountants, clerks, and so forth, differ widely in capacities, skills, training, and education. Thus, labor falls into many **noncompeting groups,** each requiring different training and receiving different wages.

Finally, some wage differences are the result of **imperfect markets.** Market imperfections include lack of information, unwillingness to move, union power, minimum-wage laws and monopsony power. The wide wage differences actually observed in the real world among different categories of people and jobs are, in general, the result of a combination of these three factors.

PRODUCTIVITY:

1. Economists consider productivity the key to prosperity. Sizable gains mean companies can pay workers more, hold the line on

prices, and still earn the kind of profits that keep stock prices rising. Increased productivity, or getting more worker output per hour on the job, is considered vital to increasing the nation's standard of living without inflation. Productivity measures the relationship between real output and the labor time involved in its production, or output per hour of work. The Labor Department compiles productivity figures from its own job surveys that produce unemployment reports and the Commerce Department's work that creates gross domestic product figures. Only business sector output—GDP minus government and not-for-profit organizations—is used in the productivity calculation.

2. Productivity measures reflect the joint effects of many influences, including changes in technology, capital investment, level of output, utilization of capacity, energy and materials, the organization of production, managerial skill, and the characteristics and effort of the work force. The data are published in a press release and in BLS journals and computer users can visit **www.stats.bls.gov** on the Internet for this data.

3. Real GDP increases when resource inputs and their productivity increase. Thus, to the extent that real GDP depends on labor inputs, real GDP equals total worker hours (labor input) times labor productivity (real output per worker per hour).

Key 70 Phillips Curve

OVERVIEW *The Phillips Curve is the curve that represents a statistical relationship between unemployment and inflation.*

Every point on the curve denotes a different combination of unemployment and inflation. It was named after A. W. Phillips, a British economist who proposed this relationship in the late 1950s.

Economic history indicates that the twin objectives of **price stability** and **full employment** (such as 4 percent unemployment rate) have been extremely difficult to achieve.

Many economists believe that there is an apparent conflict between maintaining stable prices and achieving low employment throughout the economy, due to the strong tendency for the general price level to begin to rise before full employment is reached.

Figure 1 illustrates a conventional Phillips Curve and indicates the nature of the trade-off between lower unemployment and high rates of inflation. Every point on a curve denotes a different combination of unemployment and inflation. A movement along the curve reflects the reduction in one at the expense of a gain in the other.

KEY FIGURE 1

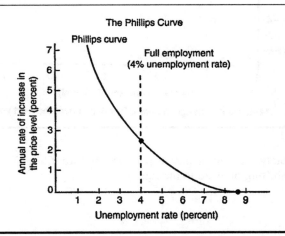

The Phillips Curve

The dilemma posed by the curve is that the economy must accept inflation in order to achieve full employment or to accept a high unemployment rate to control inflation.

To the extent that a Phillips Curve phenomenon actually exists, economic policy makers are confronted with a difficult choice of finding a fiscal-monetary mix.

Figure 2 shows statistical evidence on the tradeoff. Ideally, policy makers wish to find a policy mix that would shift the Phillips Curve downward and to the left, thus making price stability and full employment more compatible and bearable.

KEY FIGURE 2

Short-run Phillips curve 1984 to 2002

*4-quarter% change in core CPI inflation over the next year

Unfortunately, the recent past experience of **"stagflation"** shows the curve shifting outward to the right.

Key 71 Aggregate demand

OVERVIEW *Aggregate demand (AD) is the total output demanded in an economy at a given price level (over a given period of time). It is the total amount of goods people want to buy, so it does not include the unwanted output that firms produce but cannot sell.*

Aggregate demand equals the sum of the consumption, investment, government, and net export expenditures that people want to make.

The aggregate demand curve shows that aggregate demand goes up when the price level falls (Figure 1).

KEY FIGURE 1

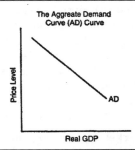

The Aggreate Demand
Curve (AD) Curve

The AD curve will shift for a change in any one of the *ceteris paribus* variables. Among the factors responsible for shifting the AD curve are changes in inflationary expectations, cash balances held by the public, government spending, taxes, and net exports.

The AD curve is a snapshot at one point in time. It does not portray a historical relationship.

The AD curve is downward sloping. This means that the public will spend more on real output at a lower average price level than at a higher price.

There are two reasons for this:
1. **Real-balance effect.** At lower prices, the purchasing power value of the public's cash balances is greater.
2. **Interest-rate effect.** When prices decline, interest rates tend to decline as well, thereby stimulating total spending.

Key 72 Equilibrium in money and goods markets

OVERVIEW *The goods market and money markets are combined to provide a comprehensive model of macroeconomic activity.*

These two markets are interrelated because of the role of money as a determinant of demand in the goods market and the concept of aggregate demand that determines the demand for money.

The linkages between the two markets may be reduced to two primary areas:

1. The interest rate is important in the goods market because we find that investment decisions are largely a function of the interest rate. For example, as interest rates increase, the cost of borrowing increases, and projects that would have been undertaken are not.
2. The interest rate may also have an impact on consumer spending to the extent that households are willing to assume higher levels of debt, thereby indirectly affecting the goods markets.

The level of **real output,** on the other hand, is a function of the level of investment; in real terms, business spending increases (decreases) must precede production increases (decreases).

Therefore, the **goods market** depends upon the interest rate, while the interest rate is itself determined in the goods market.

The **interest rate** is simply a microeconomic equilibrium between the demand for money, as determined by consumers and businesses, and the supply of money, as influenced by the Federal Reserve System.

The interrelationship between these two markets allows us to conclude that there is a unique combination of a level of real output and an interest rate that will simultaneously lead to equilibrium in each market.

Expansionary (contractionary) fiscal policy leads to increases (decreases) in interest rates because of the increase (decrease) in aggregate demand.

A potentially serious problem with increases in the interest rate associated with expansionary fiscal policy comes in the form of crowding out, which occurs when government, in an effort to follow an expansionary policy course, bids the interest rate up, making some projects unfeasible; thereby *"crowding out"* private borrowers. For example, borrowing larger than expected amounts of money, thereby forcing interest rates up.

Theoretically, monetary policy has just the opposite effect on the interest rate as that of fiscal policy. An expansionary (contractionary) monetary goal is accomplished through a reduction (increase) in the interest rate, simply because the interest rate is one of the variables that falls under the influence of the Fed. Any crowding out that occurs will have the effect of reducing the impact of the multiplier.

Key 73 Stagflation

OVERVIEW *Stagflation describes the state of the economy characterized by rising prices (inflation accompanied by insufficient expansion [stagnation]) and consequently increasing unemployment. It thus combines some of the features of inflation and recession.*

The existence of stagflation implies that a long-held tenet, the trade-off of unemployment and inflation may not be absolute, as indicated by the Phillips Curve (Key 70).

Unlike **demand-pull inflation,** stagflation does not respond to counter-inflationary monetary and fiscal measures. When the Fed and Treasury attempt to use these measures, they tend to slow down economic growth too much, causing even higher unemployment and recession.

Among the market measures for curing stagflation are:
- **Public-service job programs and various employment programs.** These programs are designed to promote the employment of the unemployed and the training of people for high-paying jobs.
- **Productivity improvement programs.** These aim at stimulating investment in physical and human capital.
- **Efforts at welfare reform.** These are designed to encourage those on welfare to seek employment.

Among the major nonmarket measures are:
- **Wage-price controls.** Part of income policies aiming at curbing inflation by setting limits in which businesses' manufacturing costs and prices may be allowed to increase.
- **Economic planning.** Programs for achieving specific economic goals through a comprehensive plan.

Key 74 Federal deficits

OVERVIEW *There has been a great deal of debate over when, if ever, the federal budget should be balanced. Keynesian economists believe that balancing the budget should have a lower priority than maintaining economic stability. However, other economists believe differently.*

By 1984, thirty-two states had passed resolutions requesting that a constitutional convention be called to draft an amendment to the United States Constitution requiring that the federal budget be balanced each year.

Some of the most frequently given arguments for a **balanced federal budget** include:
- Debt is evil.
- Debt is a burden.
- Possible inability to make the required payments.
- Debt represents government competition for resources that could be better used by the private sector.
- Financing the debt disrupts private capital markets and investment because government is competing with business for scarce resources.

These arguments are not without merit. However, it is really an argument against government spending rather than government debt, *per se*. If government spending results in unproductive national resources becoming productive, it is difficult to see how such action is taking resources away from the private sector. However, some government spending has done this.

Budget deficits can crowd out private investments. They are likely to push up interest rates and to make it more difficult for firms and others to borrow funds to finance investment projects.

Crowding out refers to the possibility that a reduction in private sector expenditures for capital goods may occur as a result of rising interest rates due to public borrowing.

To what extent financing of the federal debt by Treasury sales of bonds has discouraged private investment is not clear.

Budget deficits can be inflationary. They will push the aggregate demand curve to the right, with the result of an increased current

GDP and an increased price level. Thus, the government will have succeeded in raising current GDP, and in reducing unemployment, but this will have been achieved at the cost of considerable inflation.

The Gramm-Rudman-Hollings Act was passed by Congress and signed into law by President Reagan in December 1985. This provided for the gradual but forced reduction of the federal budget deficit to zero by the 1991 fiscal year.

The specific provisions of the bill included:
1. On August 20th, the Office of Management and Budget (OMB) and the Congressional Budget Office must jointly forecast whether the budget for the coming fiscal year meets the specified targets.
2. If it does not, the General Accounting Office (GAO) must draw up a list of across-the-board cuts, split evenly between the nonexempt military and domestic programs, that will be needed to meet the required target.
3. The list of cuts then is to be forwarded to the President, and Congress has the next thirty days to come up with an alternative plan.
4. If it does not, the President must implement the GAO list of cuts with very little flexibility.

Some questions arose regarding the constitutionality of Congress' turning over its huge responsibilities to the Congressional Budget Office, the OMB, and the GAO. These three offices represent a mixture of executive branch and legislative agencies, and it was suggested that using them is this manner might violate the separation of powers principle.

Its authors wrote a fallback provision into the bill if the part of the bill discussed above is declared unconstitutional.

If the first procedure is declared unconstitutional, the OMB, the Congressional Budget Office, and the GAO report to Congress rather than to the President.

Then, Congress is to pass a law ordering the required cuts.

The first procedure was declared unconstitutional by the United States Supreme Court in the summer of 1986.

Theme 10 INTERNATIONAL TRADE AND FINANCE

T rading in goods may be done between countries, states, and individuals for their mutual benefit. If a country has exports in excess of its imports, that country will be magnifying its income.

While free trade has advantages and disadvantages, a nation may elect to restrict trade through tariffs and import quotas. By restricting trade, the price of the item increases for the importing country resulting in less consumption. Such restrictions may be made to protect a new industry, or to protect national security.

The balance of payments is a mathematical tabulation of a country's transactions with other countries. These transactions include exports and imports of goods and services, investments, currency, gold, and gifts. An imbalance may be corrected by changing prices and/or interest rates. A government may intervene to influence the exchange rate depending on national objectives.

Key 75 Gains from trade

OVERVIEW *The critical factor that derives gains in trade is interdependency.*

Each trading entity specializes in its comparative advantage. By doing so, each entity yields a greater quantity of a product than the sum of the two entities production alone.

The **law of comparative advantage** is the fundamental reason for trading. It is when two entities, each one producing the same two types of goods, specialize in one good that it can produce at a lower opportunity cost. Therefore, both entities derive more goods by trading because each entity can offer the best produced good at the best possible price.

Any two entities can engage in trade, i.e. two nations, two states, or two persons.

Example: If two entities were independent then there would be no reason to trade. Each entity would produce on the basis of its needs. For instance, the United States produces 20 units of meat and 20 units of wine, and France produces 20 units of meat and 30 units of wine. Each country then specializes in the product where it has the comparative advantage and trades for the other product. Now, the United States produces 60 units of meat and 0 unit of wine. France produces 90 units of wine and 0 unit of meat. The two countries trade 30 units.

Country	Pre-Trade		Post-Trade		Net Gain	
	Meat	Wine	Meat	Wine	Meat	Wine
U.S.	20	20	60	0	20	0
France	20	30	0	90	0	40

Key 76 Foreign trade multiplier

OVERVIEW *The foreign trade multiplier is a concept that states that the net exports (exports minus imports) may magnify the impact on the nation's income.*

The **"bathtub theorem"** operates as follows:
1. **Exports** are "injections" such as government spending and investment that have positive effects on the national income level. Thus, injections raise the water-level of the bathtub.
2. **Imports** are "withdrawals" or "leakages," such as savings and taxes, that have negative effects on the national income level. Thus, withdrawals lower the water-level of the bathtub.
3. **Neutral effect.** Exports equals imports, thus GDP does not change. In bathtub terms, injections are equal to withdrawals keeping the water-level the same.
4. **Expansionary effect.** Exports are greater than imports, thus GDP increases. In bathtub terms, injections are greater than withdrawals raising the water-level of the bathtub.
5. **Contractionary effect.** Exports are less than imports, thus GDP decreases. In bathtub terms, injections are less than withdrawals lowering the water-level of the bathtub.

Imports depend on the level of national income. As the national income increases, so do domestic expenditures on imports. Thus, Marginal Propensity to Import (*MPM*) is defined as:

$$\text{MPM} = \frac{\text{Change in imports}}{\text{Change in income}}$$

Exports have no relationship with the level of national income, thus they are independent.

With the assumptions described above, an increase in exports tends to raise domestic income, but the increased income also encourages some imports, which act as "leakages." These tend to reduce the full multiplier effect that would exist if imports remained constant.

Open economy's allocation of income is $MPC + MPS + MPM = 1$. Thus, *MPM* is the fraction of any increase in income that "leaks" into imports.

The **foreign-trade multiplier** is defined as the reciprocal of all the leak-ages, including imports.

$$\text{Foreign-trade multiplier} = \frac{1}{MPS + MPM} = \frac{1}{\text{leakage}}$$

If *MPS* is constant then the *MPM* has an inverse relationship with *MPC*. As more imports are consumed, there are smaller amounts to be consumed for domestic goods.

Example: If the *MPS* = 0.15 and the *MPM* = .05, the total leakage is .20. Therefore,

$$\text{Foreign-trade multiplier} = 1/(0.15+0.05) = 5$$

One unit change in aggregate expenditure will have a five unit change in GDP.

In contrast, the simple multiplier for a closed economy is $1/.15 = 6.67$.

Key 77 Case for free trade

OVERVIEW *In trade, two fundamental concepts are absolute advantage and comparative advantage.*

Absolute advantage is when one nation can produce a product more efficiently than the other. Thus, a basis of trade is created.

Comparative advantage allows even a nation that can produce two goods more efficiently to establish a basis for trade.

The law of absolute advantage states that when two nations specialize in the products that each can produce more efficiently, a basis for trade is established. Thus, both nations can obtain the two goods at lower opportunity cost.

Example: the United States has an absolute advantage in computers while Brazil has an absolute advantage in coffee. By specializing, the United States and Brazil respectively obtain computers and coffee at lower opportunity cost.

If one nation has a **lower opportunity cost** for two goods than the other nation, then a basis for trade may still be established. The key concept is comparative advantage. Each nation should specialize in the product that has the lowest opportunity cost.

Example: A lawyer may be a good typist, but the lawyer may find that time would be best spent on practicing law rather than typing. Thus, employing a less efficient typist may be advantageous.

The principle that governs the lawyer-typist relationship applies to countries as well. By restricting free trade, each country's production-possibility curve shifts to the left. In effect, each nation is not at its maximum efficiency.

Through specialization and free trade, nations can achieve a more efficient allocation of scarce world resources, thereby raising standards of living.

Key 78 Case for restricted trade

OVERVIEW *Restrictions on trade take the following forms: tariffs, import quotas, and nontariff barriers.*

The economic consequences of import restrictions are almost the same as those resulting from an increase in transportation costs. Such costs raise prices in the importing country and reduce the volume of goods consumed.

Quotas reduce competition. Quota allocation may be abused.

Tariffs create tax revenues for the importing nation, which are distributed and raise prices of imports thus reducing demand for the product. However, tariffs still allow market forces to react.

If a protective measure must be placed, then a tariff would be better than a quota.

Imports create jobs. An exporting nation increases income derived from trade and buys from the importing nation with the income derived from trade. Thus, the importing nation creates jobs in industries that export to the exporting nation.

Protection reduces exports. By reducing imports, internal employment is produced. However, the restriction reduces the income of the exporting nations. In effect, other nations will not have as much income to buy the imports. Thus, employment in exporting industries will be reduced.

Protection reduces consumer choice. Import restriction reduces the spectrum of products. Thus, the consumers are not able to buy "the best value for their money."

Protection reduces competition. By reducing foreign competition, domestic companies have a carte blanche to be less efficient and to gain monopolistic control.

Key 79 Arguments for protection

OVERVIEW *Opposition for the law of comparative advantage and economic gains from trade have made many arguments to refute free trade.*

The **infant-industry argument:**
1. An infant industry, an underdeveloped industry, is usually protected by tariffs or quotas. The protection is effective until the industry is technologically advanced and efficient enough to compete with its foreign competition.
2. Protective measures, i.e. tariffs, tend to be vested by special interests. Thus, they are very difficult to remove.
3. Some infant industries never grow out of infancy.
4. Tariffs and quotas raise prices for domestic consumers. A subsidy is more effective and results in lower prices.

The **national-security argument:**
1. Some industries are important for the defense industry. Protection for these industries may be warranted. However, this argument is a defense issue not an economic one.
2. The better method of protection would be subsidizing vital industries, i.e. steel.

The **wage-protection argument:**
1. Wages in the United States are higher than in other countries. Therefore, the need for tariffs and quotas are presented to protect American workers' wages and standard of living.
2. Industries can be categorized as labor-, capital-, and land-intensive. Low wage countries have advantages for labor-intensive industries.
3. Even a high wage country may be competitive if its productivity is able to make up for the higher wages.

The **employment-protection argument:**
1. The employment-protection argument says that import restrictions will lead to increased domestic production, employment and income.
2. Tariffs and quotas lead to retaliation, thus both sides lose.
3. Tariffs and quotas shift domestic resources from more efficient to protected ones to compensate for reduced imports, thus raising domestic prices.
4. Trade involves export and import. Restricted import results in restricted export.

Key 80 Balance of payments

OVERVIEW *The balance of payments is a statistical tabulation of all kinds of a nation's transactions with all other countries during a given period—usually a year.*

These transactions consist of exports and imports of goods and services, and movements of short-term and long-term investments, currency, gold, and gifts. The transactions may be classified into several categories, of which the two major ones are the **current account** and the **capital account.**

Balance of payments is a double-entry accounting of the money value of all exchanges and transfers of goods, services, capital loans, and gold and international reserves between the individual residents, businesses, and government of one nation and the rest of the world for a given time (usually one year).

All entries are either debits (payments) or credits (receipts), whether or not actual payment is made during the period in question; it is the claim for payment that counts.

A debit for one nation automatically represents a credit for another; if an American family visits France and spends $1,000 there, it creates a $1,000 debit for the U.S. balance of payments and a $1,000 credit for the French balance of payments.

A nation's balance of payments is divided into three accounts:
1. The **current account** consists of commodity exports, re- exports, and imports (visible items of trade, or merchandise), and services such as tourism, banking, insurance, and transportation, profits earned abroad, and interest (invisible items of trade). It also includes unilateral transfers, that is, one-way transactions such as grants of foreign aid or individual gifts. The difference between the total export of goods and services and the total imports is called the balance on current account. The difference between total goods (merchandise only) imported and exported is the balance of trade.
2. The **capital account** consists of the inward and outward flow of investment capital. It usually is subdivided into long-term and short-term capital flows, based on when claims fall due (if in a year or more, long-term; otherwise, short-term). Short-term classifications include bank deposits, call loans, short-term govern-

ment bonds, and currency holdings; long-term categories include bond issues sold abroad and direct investment in foreign plant and equipment.

In the **double-entry system**, payment must always balance over a given period, that is, debits must equal credits. If the combined capital and current accounts show a deficit (with more goods and services and/or capital investment coming into a nation than going out), the difference is made up by the third account, the reserve and gold account, which consists of compensatory gold and reserves movements.

3. Thus, if a nation's debits exceed its credits, it must either export gold or spend some if its foreign-currency reserves (usually U.S. dollars) to meet its obligations; if, on the other hand, it has a surplus (credits exceed debits), the statement is brought into balance by an inflow of gold and reserves. Since the creation of Special Drawing Rights (sometimes called "paper gold") on the International Monetary Fund, these have become an important means of offsetting a deficit.

The **balance of trade** is the difference between a nation's imports and exports of merchandise to and from all other countries over a given period.

If exports exceed imports, the balance of trade is said to be favorable and the nation has a trade surplus; if imports exceed exports, it is unfavorable.

Merchandise transactions make up the major part of the current account of a nation's balance of payments.

An **unfavorable balance of trade**, more often called a trade deficit results when the opposite is the case.

A large **trade deficit** could drive interest rates higher resulting in lower stock prices and lower currency prices as the country increases its reliance on foreign capital to finance the budget deficit.

Key 81 Foreign exchange market

OVERVIEW *The foreign exchange market is a market where foreign exchange transactions take place; that is, where different currencies are bought and sold. In practice this market is not located in any one place, most transactions being conducted by telephone, wire service, or cable.*

The three functions of the foreign exchange market are to **transfer purchasing power, provide credit,** and **minimize exchange risk.**

The market is dominated by banks; nonbank foreign exchange dealers; individuals and firms conducting commercial and investment transactions; and exchange brokers who buy and sell foreign currencies, making a profit on the difference between the exchange rates and interest rates among the various world financial centers.

In addition to the settlement of obligations incurred through investment, purchases, and other trading, the foreign exchange market involves speculation in exchange futures. New York and London are the major centers for these transactions.

Key 82 Flexible versus fixed

exchange rates and strong dollar

versus weak dollar

OVERVIEW *Foreign exchange is an instrument used for international payment.*

Instruments of foreign currency consist not only of currency, but also of checks, drafts, and bills of exchange.

A **foreign exchange market** is available for trading foreign exchanges.

A **foreign exchange rate** is the price of one currency in terms of another. For example, one American dollar is 135 yen in Japanese currency.

Fixed exchange rates result from an international financial arrangement in which governments directly intervene in the foreign exchange market to prevent exchange rates from deviating more than a very small margin from some central or parity value.

Flexible rates derive from an arrangement by which exchange rate levels are allowed to change daily in response to market demand and supply. Arrangements may vary from **free float**, that is, absolutely no government intervention, to **managed float**, that is, limited but sometimes aggressive government intervention in the foreign exchange market.

The **forward rate** is the contracted exchange rate for receipt of and payment for foreign currency at a specified date, usually 30 days, 90 days, or 180 days in the future, at a stipulated current or "spot" price.

By buying and selling forward exchange contracts, importers and exporters can protect themselves against the risks of fluctuations in the current exchange market.

STRONG DOLLAR AND WEAK DOLLAR:
What is better, a strong dollar or a weak dollar? The answer is, unfortunately, it depends. A strong dollar makes Americans' cash go further overseas and reduces import prices—generally good for U.S. consumers and for foreign manufacturers. If the dollar is overvalued, U.S. products are harder to sell abroad and at home, where they compete with low-cost imports. This helps give the United States its huge

trade deficit. A weak dollar can restore competitiveness to American products by making foreign goods comparatively more expensive. But too weak a dollar can spawn inflation, first through higher import prices and then through spiraling prices for all goods. Even worse, a falling dollar can drive foreign investors away from U.S. securities, which lose value along with the dollar. A strong dollar can be induced by interest rates. Relatively higher interest rates abroad will attract money dollar-denominated investments that will raise the value of the dollar. Those Americans owning foreign investments must watch the dollar carefully. A weak dollar makes overseas investments more valuable since assets sold in the foreign currency will yield more dollars. Conversely, a strong dollar will hurt the values of an American's overseas holdings. Assets priced overseas in these scenarios would mean less dollars than to the depressed local currency. The table below summarizes the impacts of changes in foreign exchange rates on various aspects of the economy.

THE IMPACTS OF CHANGES IN FOREIGN EXCHANGE RATES

	Weak Currency *(Depreciation/devaluation)*	*Strong Currency* *(Appreciation/revaluation)*
Imports	More expensive	Cheaper
Exports	Cheaper	More expensive
Payables	More expensive	Cheaper
Receivables	Cheaper	More expensive
Inflation	Fuel inflation by making imports more costly	Low inflation
Foreign investment	Discourage foreign investment. Lower return on investments by international investors.	High interest rates could attract foreign investors.
The effect	Rising interests could slow down the economy.	Reduced exports could trigger a trade deficit.

Key 83 Correcting a persistent
payments deficit

OVERVIEW   *There are three forces that will lead to alleviation of a country's payments imbalance: A rise in the home country's price of imports; a fall in the foreign country's price of exports; and a possible rise in interest rates.*

In the event of a **depreciation** of a currency, that currency will, of course, purchase fewer units of foreign currency, and imports will thus become more expensive to domestic consumers.

If the dollar depreciates, the dollar amount of U.S. expenditure on imports will fall if demand is elastic, but will rise if demand is inelastic.

From the viewpoint of the United States, there is a rightward shift of the foreign demand curve for U.S. exports. Thus, both the dollar price and the quantity demanded of U.S. exports increase. This will occur as long as foreign demand for U.S. exports is not totally inelastic.

The **Marshall-Lerner condition** states that depreciation of a currency will result in an excess of exports over imports for the depreciating country if the sum of the elasticities of the home and foreign demands is greater than one. This assumes that supply elasticities are infinite, and that the trade balance was zero before the depreciation.

Since currency depreciation has inflationary effects, the monetary authorities of a country undergoing depreciation may choose to use contractionary monetary policy. If so, there will be a rise in interest rates that will attract a short-term capital inflow. This capital inflow will also help to cure the payments imbalance.

Conflict will occur between external and internal policies in cases where a country has a balance of payments deficit during a period of internal recession.

Contractionary monetary and fiscal policies are appropriate to cure the trade deficit but recession calls for expansionary monetary and fiscal policies.

One way to reduce pressures toward currency depreciation is to restrict imports, as well as to place special taxes on interest or dividends from foreign investment.

Such policies tend to disrupt trade and resource allocation and are not widely favored by economists.

Theme 11 ISSUES IN MACROECONOMICS

*T*he classical model assumes the operation of a free-enterprise, highly competitive economic system. Prices will adjust to changes in demand and supply. Keynesian economics is under the premise that an economy may be in equilibrium at any employment level, not necessarily at full employment, and active fiscal and monetary policies are required to seek economic expansion with stable prices.

Under the monetarism theory, changes in monetary growth are the major reasons for change in the price level and GDP. Neoclassical economics is also called the marginalist school and assumes pure competition with many buyers and sellers, uniform prices, and homogeneous products.

Rational expectation theory is a belief that people's expectations of future conditions have an impact on present economic behavior. Supply-side economics attempts to accomplish efficiency with economic policies and measures designed to stimulate production. Demand-side economics stresses the regulation of aggregate demand.

Key 84 Classical (market clearing) model

OVERVIEW *The classical model assumes the operation of a free-enterprise, highly competitive economic system. This is a system in which there are many buyers and sellers, both in product markets and in resource markets.*

The **classical model** is a system in which all prices are flexible so that they can quickly adjust upward or downward to changing supplies and demands in the marketplace. In this type of economic system, the product and resource markets will automatically adjust to full-employment levels as if guided by an "invisible hand." This is because aggregate expenditure equals aggregate income or output.

There are two propositions of classical economics:
1. The economy operates at the full- or natural-employment level. The volume of output produced at this level is the economy's potential output, also called potential real GDP.
2. The average price level is flexible. Output is independent of prices, as indicated by the fact that the same potential real GDP is produced at a relatively low price level as at a relatively high one.

Key 85 Keynesianism

OVERVIEW *Keynesian economics is a body of economic thought and principles that originated with the British Economist John Maynard Keynes (1882–1946) in the 1930s. It has since been modified, extended, and empirically tested to the point where many of its basic prescriptions, ideas, and tools are now an integral part of general economic theory and governmental economic policy.*

Through his book *The General Theory of Employment, Interest and Money* (1936), Keynes contends that an economy may be in equilibrium at any level of employment, not necessarily at full employment, and therefore, active fiscal and monetary policies are needed to seek full employment and economic growth with price stability.

In addition, Keynesian economics focuses on stimulating aggregate demand and thus has been referred to as **demand-side economics.**

Keynesian economics stresses:
- The dependency of consumption on income, called the consumption function.
- The multiplier effect of an autonomous spending on GDP.
- The marginal efficiency of investment as a measure of business demand for investment.

Key 86 Monetarism

OVERVIEW *Monetarism is a theory of the relationship between changes in the growth rate in money supply and changes in the price level. It postulates that change in the monetary growth rate is the primary cause of change in the price level, and hence changes in nominal GDP (Key 63).*

Monetarists believe that the marginal propensity to consume varies a great deal from year to year—so much so that we cannot predict the effect of a change in government spending because we cannot accurately predict the true value of the multiplier during any specific given period.

They view the relationship between the quantity of money and national income as more stable because, like the classical economists, they believe that the velocity of money is nearly constant in the short run. Thus, to the extent that they are willing to use either fiscal or monetary policy, they favor monetary policy.

However, many monetarists, like classical economists, believe that if left to itself, an economy will always eventually work its way back to full employment through flexible wages and prices.

They see government policies such as minimum wage rates and licensing requirements as only hindering this process. In fact, some monetarists believe that discretionary government fiscal and monetary policies tend to destabilize the economy.

In a Keynesian model, an increase in the money supply lowers the rate of interest; this reduced borrowing cost raises investment spending, which causes a multiple increase in the level of income. Figure 1 presents a Keynesian view of the transmission process.

Monetarists view money as one of many assets households and businesses hold in a portfolio of assets. Any change in its quantity affects the demand for other assets in the portfolio. Thus, an increase in the money supply raises the demand for other assets. This increases the amount spent on capital investment, consumer durable goods, residential housing and a host of other private sector goods and services. Figure 2 presents a monetarist's view of the transmission process.

Monetarists consider money unique and hold that its demand is stable and insensitive to the rate of interest. Keynesians contend that money has many close substitutes, and that the demand for money is variable. Given these views, monetarists argue that the velocity of money (v) is stable and predictable;

Keynesians believe that V is variable. Monetary policy has a predictable effect upon the nominal level of income according to the monetarists; Keynesians suggest that the effect of money supply changes is variable.

Monetarists consider the market the best allocator of resources and output. Since monetary policy affects spending through the market, money supply changes are considered the best policy variable.

Keynesians, however, see a need for government interference to overcome problems of social imbalance and the unequal distribution of income. Such objectives can be promoted by tax and/or government spending changes while the government is also trying to stabilize the level of income.

Monetarists contend that fiscal measures are weak; they argue that stimulative fiscal measures force up the rate of interest and "crowd out" private investment.

KEY FIGURE 1

Money supply ↑ → Rate of interest ↓ → Level of investment spending ↑ → Level of consumer spending ↑ → Level of income ↑

KEY FIGURE 2

Money supply ↑ → Spending on capital goods, consumer durable goods, residential housing, and the like ↑ → Level of income ↑

Key 87 Neoclassical macroeconomics

OVERVIEW *Neoclassical economics is often called the marginalist school. It is a group of economists whose ideas dominated Western economic thought from the 1870s to the 1930s, first replacing classical economics and then being considerably modified by Keynesian economics (Key 84).*

Like the classical school, **neoclassical economics** hypothesized a state of pure competition, with many buyers and sellers, many homogeneous products, uniform prices, and no special influences on prices such as might be exerted by monopoly, advertising, and the like.

Such a market, they thought, tended toward a perfect equilibrium, so like the classical economists, the marginalists believed that government should not interfere with markets.

They assumed that an economic man generally behaved rationally, minimizing pain and maximizing pleasure.

They were primarily concerned with refining the principles of price and allocation theory, **"marginalism,"** the theory of capital, and related aspects of economics.

Like Adam Smith and other classical economists, Alfred Marshall believed in an underlying equilibrium of the market. Sooner or later demand and supply must meet in a **"normal price,"** and this process is self-adjusting, requiring no outside interference to make it happen.

Business cycles—the ups and downs of the overall economy—are simply temporary deviations from the ultimate norm.

Marshall believed in the **Quantity Theory of Money,** and he devised an equation to explain this relationship.

Key 88 Rational expectations

OVERVIEW *Rational expectations is a belief that maintains that people's expectations about the future, based on current information and their understanding of the economy, deeply affect current economic behavior.*

Its leaders, notably Robert Lucas, Thomas Sargent, and Patrick Minford, therefore believe government should work to provide a stable environment for business and consumers by following firm, long-term moderate policies on which people can rely. Shifts in fiscal or monetary policy cannot increase output and employment.

Under the **Rational Expectations Theory**, individuals and businesses utilize information efficiently. Thus, they analyze and forecast prices, interest rates, money supply, and other key economic variables, and then make decisions based on those forecasts.

Widely expected policy moves have no impact when made because they have already been incorporated into people's decisions.

The only policy moves that can change people's behavior are the ones that are not expected, that is, surprise moves.

Therefore, to ensure economic stability, government should choose the right policy and adhere to it. This implies that the government should stick to a policy of balanced budgets and a growth of the money supply. Otherwise, it will be self-defeating and inflationary.

According to the **New Classical View,** demand and supply function will adequately regulate prices and wages, and those who want jobs will find them because they will, if necessary, settle for lower pay. This view is sometimes called new classical economics because, like the older classical school, it stresses free market forces.

These views are opposed by the new Keynesians, who support more government control over the economy—to boost demand during a recession, for example.

Most new Keynesians, such as Laurence Klein, Sir John Hicks, James Tobin, and James Meade, agree that people's expectations may be rational, but because wages are rigid, owing to wage laws and strong unions, supply and demand cannot balance fast enough for all workers to find jobs.

Key 89 Supply-side economics

OVERVIEW *Supply-side economics aims at achieving efficiency through economic policies and measures designed to stimulate production.*

On the other hand, **demand-side economics** focuses on regulating aggregate demand. Keynesian economics, because it tends to focus on fiscal and monetary policies to control aggregate demand, has been characterized as demand-side economics.

Supply-side economics relies heavily on the direct use of incentives. For example, reductions in marginal tax rates—the taxes paid on the last dollar of taxable income—provide direct incentives to work, save, and invest, thereby stimulating aggregate supply rather than aggregate demand.

Tight monetary control to curb inflation is another principal prescription of supply-side economics.

The **Laffer Curve**—named after a supply-side economist, Arthur Laffer—shows a hypothetical relationship between the marginal tax rate and tax revenues.

As Figure 1 indicates, as the tax rate increases from 0 to 100 percent, tax revenues rise from 0 to some maximum level and then decline to 0.

The optimum tax rate is, of course, the one that reaches the maximum revenue. Rates that are lower than optimum are regarded "normal" because tax revenues can be increased by raising the rate. Rates that are above optimum are viewed as prohibitive because they dampen incentives on the parts of businesses and individuals and are thus counterproductive.

Therefore, when the rate is in the prohibitive range, reductions in tax are needed to provide incentives, stimulate production, and bring higher, not lower, tax revenues.

There is no empirical evidence to support this relationship and it still remains a hypothesis.

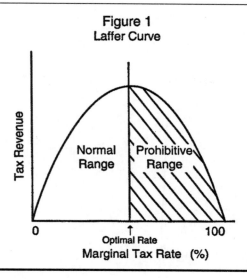

Figure 1
Laffer Curve

GLOSSARY

Included here are the definitions of many, but not all, of the terms used in the Keys. For terms not listed here, please consult the index.

absolute advantage Ability to produce a good with fewer resources per unit than that of its trading partners.

accelerationist hypothesis The hypothesis that an accelerating rate of inflation is necessary to reduce unemployment below its natural rate.

accelerator principle The principle that net investment depends on changes in GDP.

aggregate demand schedule Schedule that relates aggregate demand to various price levels.

aggregate supply schedule Schedule that relates aggregate supply to various price levels.

automatic stabilizers A tax or expenditure designed to provide a countercyclical impetus to the economy.

average propensity to consume (APC) The ratio of consumption expenditures to disposable income.

average propensity to save (APS) The ratio of personal saving to disposable income.

balance of payments accounts Accounts used to record the international transactions of a country.

balance of payments deficit The amount by which the quantity of a currency supplied exceeds the amount demanded.

business cycle A pattern of ups and downs in the output of goods and services.

comparative advantage The ability to produce a good at a lower opportunity cost.

cost-push inflation Inflation caused by an increase in the cost of one or more resources.

cyclical unemployment Unemployment caused by downswings of the business cycle.

circular flow model A simplified picture of the integrated flow of resources, goods, and services among broad sectors of the economy.

consumption function Mathematical relationship showing consumption at different levels of disposable income.

crowding out Decreases in private investment spending (which is mainly financed by borrowing) resulting from increases in government borrowing.

current account Balance of payments account keeping track of all the national international transactions of goods and services.

demand-pull inflation Inflation caused by an increase in the nation's demand for goods that exceeds its ability to produce the goods at stable prices.

disposable income After-tax household income available for spending.

equation of exchange Nominal GDP must equal the money supply times its velocity, or $MV = PQ$.

equilibrium A state in which all forces or variables are balanced.

equilibrium GDP Level of GDP when aggregate demand is equal to aggregate supply.

expenditure multiplier The change in the equilibrium level of real GDP for a change in planned aggregate expenditures.

expenditures approach A system for measuring GDP by summing up expenditures on final goods and services by households, businesses, governments, and net exports.

equilibrium in aggregate demand When spending equals income or when leakages equal injections.

euro The European currency that replaced national currencies in 11 countries in 2002.

federal debt The amount the government owes to creditors.

federal deficit Excess of government spending over taxes collected for a year.

Federal Reserve System The U.S. central bank.

financial intermediaries Institutions that borrow funds from savers and loan them to other individuals or institutions.

fiscal policy The government's use of taxes and expenditures to achieve desired economic goals.

flexible (floating) exchange rate An exchange rate that is set by free market forces without government intervention.

foreign exchange rate The price of one nation's currency in terms of another nation's currency.

frictional unemployment Unemployment due to normal shifts in job turnover, or routine business closings.

full employment Employment of 93 or 96 percent of the labor force.

GDP gap gap between actual and potential output.

Gross Domestic Product (GDP) total money value of all final goods and services produced by an economy (within its boundaries) during a year.

income approach A system for measuring GDP by summing factor payments by businesses to households (income).

inflation An increase in the general level of prices.

inflation rate Percent increase in price level over a year.

injections Any form of spending other than consumption. Includes investment and government spending.

Keynesian theory A theory proposed by J.M. Keynes that assumes prices are rigid and real output adjusts to changes in expenditures.

leakage A withdrawal or outflow of income that is not directly spent on goods and services. Includes taxes, imports, and savings.

M1 Measure of the money supply counting only cash held by the public plus checking accounts.

Marginal Efficiency of Capital (MEC) The annual rate of return, on each additional dollar of investment expenditure.

Marginal Propensity to Consume (MPC) added consumption due to $1 more of disposable income.

Marginal Propensity to Save (MPS) The change in saving for a dollar change in disposable income.

modified Phillips Curve The curve that plots the change in the inflation rate against the unemployment rate; also called an *expectations-augmented Phillips Curve* or an *accelerationist Phillips Curve*.

monetarist theory Theory that stresses the link between the money supply and the price level.

monetary policy policy manipulating the rate of growth of the nation's money supply to achieve desired economic goals.

money Any generally accepted medium of exchange.

net investment Equals gross investment minus depreciation.

Net Domestic Product (NDP) A monetary measure of the net value of final goods and services produced in the economy during a year. GDP minus depreciation.

new economy The notion that rapid technological advance in the information technology (IT) sector is fundamentally changing the nature of the U.S. economy.

nominal GDP The value of final goods and services produced during a given year, using that year's prices. Also referred to as "GNP in current dollars."

Okun's law A law that states that an annual 2.5 percent increase in the rate of real growth above trend growth results in a 1 percent decrease in the unemployment rate.

open market operation A major method used by the Fed to change money supply. The buying and selling of government securities by the Federal Open Market Committee (FOMC).

personal consumption Household spending on consumer goods.

personal income A measure of income available to households.

Phillips Curve Curve showing a trade-off between inflation and unemployment.

potential GDP An estimate of attainable GDP, if unemployment equals 4 percent.

Price Index A means to measure changes in the general price level over time by comparing the cost of specified items.

Production Possibilities Curve A curve illustrating the various combinations of goods that a society is capable of producing at any given time if its technology and resources are fixed and all its resources are fully and efficiently employed.

Quantity theory of money Classical theory of the relationship between the price level and the money supply. It uses the equation of exchange for prediction purposes.

rational expectations An approach to economics that claims that anticipations are based on both past experience and a reasoned analysis of available information.

real GDP The value of final goods and services produced during a given year, valued at the price level for some base year. GDP expressed in constant dollars.

recession A decline in GDP that lasts for at least two consecutive quarters.

reserve ratio Fraction of their deposits that banks must keep at the Federal Reserve Bank.

spending multiplier Number by which an initial increase in spending must be multiplied to get the resulting change in GDP.

stagflation Combination of high rates of inflation and recession.

structural unemployment Unemployment caused by changes in the structure of industry.

supply-side economics An approach to economics that aims at achieving efficiency through policies designed to stimulate production.

tax multiplier Relation between a change in personal income taxes and the resulting change in GDP. A tax multiplier of −5 implies that a $100 increase in taxes will reduce GDP by $500.

transaction demand for money Money demand due to money holdings

unemployment rate Percent of the labor force that is unemployed.

velocity The average number of times a year that a dollar is used during a given year.

APPENDIX

UNDERSTANDING ECONOMIC DATA AND INDICATORS

*M*anagers and entrepreneurs must keep abreast of the economic trend and direction and attempt to see how they affect their businesses. Investors have to cut through all the economic indicators and statistical data so that they can make informed investment decisions. Unfortunately, there are too many economic indicators and variables to be analyzed. Each has its own significance. In many cases, these variables could give mixed signals about the future of the economy.

Various government agencies and private firms tabulate the appropriate economic data and calculate various indices. Sources for these indicators are easily subscribed to at an affordable price or can be found in your local public and college libraries. They include daily local newspapers and national newspapers such as *USA Today, Wall Street Journal, Investor's Business Daily, Los Angeles Times,* and *New York Times*, and periodicals such as *Business Week, Forbes, Fortune, Money, Worth, Barron's, Smart Money, Nation's Business,* and *US News and World Report*. Internet users can look at the White House web site's Economic Statistics Briefing Room that provides easy access to current federal economic indicators. The Briefing Room is at *www.whitehouse.gov/fsbr/esbr.html*.

Economic Indicators and Stocks and Businesses

The accompanying chart summarizes the types of economic variables and their probable effect on the security market and the economy in general.

Economic Variables	Impact on Security Market and Businesses
Real growth in GDP	Positive (without inflation) for stocks and businesses.
Industrial production	Consecutive drops are a sign of recession. Bad for stocks and businesses.
Inflation	Detrimental to stocks and businesses.
Capacity utilization	A high percentage is positive, but full capacity is inflationary.
Durable goods orders	Consecutive drops are a sign of recession. Very bad for stocks and businesses in cyclical industries.
Increase in business investment, consumer confidence, personal income, etc.	Positive for businesses, especially retailing. Worrisome for utility companies.
Leading indicators	Rise is bullish for the economy and businesses; drops are a sign of bad times ahead
Housing starts	Rise is positive for housing businesses.
Corporate profits	Strong corporate earnings are positive for businesses; corporate bonds also fare well.
Unemployment	Upward trend unfavorable for businesses and economy.
Increase in business inventories	Positive for those fearful of inflationary; Negative for those looking for growing economy
Lower federal deficit	Lowers interest rates, good for many businesses. Potential negative for depressed economy
Deficit in trade and balance of payments	Negative for economy and businesses of companies facing stiff import competition
Weak dollar	Negative for economy; good for companies with stiff foreign competition.
Interest rates	Rising rates can choke off investment in new plants and lure skittish investors from businesses.

The accompanying chart merely serves as a handy guide and should not be construed as an accurate predictor in all cases. Many times the anticipation of good or bad news is built into the market and when the news comes out, the reverse move happens. That is because traders are unwinding the positions they took to profit from that news.

Economic Indicators and Bond Yields

The bond investor makes an analysis of the economy primarily to determine his or her investment strategy. It is not necessary for the investor to formulate his or her own economic forecasts. The accompanying chart provides a concise and brief list of the significant economic indicators and how they affect bond yields.

Indicators*	Effects on Bond Yields**	Reasons
Business Activity		
GDP and industrial production falls	Fall	As economy slows, Fed may ease credit by allowing rates to fall
Unemployment rises	Fall	High unemployment indicates lack of economic expansion. Fed may loosen credit
Inventories rise	Fall	Inventory levels are good indicators of duration of economic slowdown
Trade deficit rises	Fall	Dollar weakens. That's inflationary.
Leading indicators	Rise	Advance signals about economic health; Fed may tighten credit
Housing starts rise	Rise	Growing economy due to increased new housing demand; Fed may tighten; mortgage rates rise
Personal income rises	Rise	Higher income means higher consumer spending, thus inflationary; Fed may tighten
Inflation		
Consumer Price Index	Rise	Inflationary rises
Producer Price Index	Rise	Early signal for inflation increase
Monetary Policy		
Money supply rises	Rise	Excess growth in money supply is inflationary; Fed may tighten

Fed funds rate rises	Rise	Increase in business and consumer loan rates; used by Fed to slow economic growth and inflation
Fed buys (sells) bills	Rise (fall)	Adds (deduct) money to the economy; interest rates may go down (up)
Required reserve rises	Rise	Depresses banks' lending

* This table merely serves as a handy guide and should not be construed as accurate at all times.

** Fall in any of these indicators will have the opposite effect on bond yields.

Note: The effects are based on yield and are therefore opposite of how bond prices will be affected.

Economic Indicator: Index of Leading Indicators

The Index of Leading Indicators is the economic series of indicators that tends to predict future changes in economic activity. This index was designed to reveal the direction of the economy in the next six to nine months. By melding 10 economic yardsticks, an index is created that has shown a tendency to change before the economy makes a major turn; hence, the term "leading indicators." The index is designed to forecast economic activity six to nine months ahead.

This series is calculated and published monthly by the Conference Board, consisting of:

1. **Average weekly hours for U.S. manufacturing workers.** Employers find it a lot easier to increase the number of hours worked in a week than to hire more employees.
2. **Average weekly initial claims for unemployment insurance.** The number of people who sign up for unemployment benefits signals changes in present and future economic activity.
3. **Manufacturers' new orders, consumer goods and materials.** New orders mean more workers hired, more materials and supplies purchased, and increased output. Gains in this series usually lead recoveries by as much as four months.
4. **Vendor performance, slower deliveries diffusion index.** Represents the percentage of companies reporting slower

deliveries. As the economy grows, firms have more trouble filling orders.

5. **Manufacturers' new orders, nondefense capital goods.** Factories will employ more as demand for big-ticket items, especially those not bought by the government, stays strong.

6. **Building permits, new private housing units.** Optimistic builders often a good sign for the economy.

7. **Stock prices, 500 common stocks.** Stock market advances usually precede business upturns by three to eight months.

8. **Money supply, M2.** A rising money supply means easy money that sparks brisk economic activity. This usually leads recoveries by as much as fourteen months.

9. **Interest rate spread, 10-year Treasury bonds minus federal funds rate.** Steep yield curve, when long rates are much higher than short ones, is sign of healthy economic outlook.

10. **Consumer expectations index.** Consumer spending buys two-thirds of GDP (all goods and services produced in the economy), so any sharp change could be an important factor in an overall turnaround.

The monthly report is well covered by daily business publications, major newspapers, business TV shows and on the Internet. You can also check the Conference Board's web site at *www.conference-board.com*. If the index is consistently rising, even only slightly, the economy is chugging along and a setback is unlikely. If the indicator drops for three or more consecutive months, look for an economic slowdown and possibly a recession in the next year or so. A rising indicator is bullish for the economy and the stock market, and vice versa. Falling index results could be good news for bondholders looking to make capital gains from falling interest rates. Now the Conference Board points out that while it is often stated in the press that three consecutive downward movements in the leading index signal a recession, they do not endorse the use of such a simple, inflexible rule. Their studies show that a 1 percent decline (2 percent when annualized) in the leading index, coupled with declines in a majority of the 10 components, provides a reliable, but not perfect, recession signal. *Note:* The composite figure is designed to tell only in which direction business will go. It is not intended to forecast the magnitude of future ups and downs. The index has also given some false warning signals in recent years.

Coincident indicators. These are the types of economic indicator series that tend to move up and down in line with the aggregate economy and therefore are measures of current economic activity. Examples are Gross Domestic Product (GDP), retail sales, and industrial production.

Lagging indicators. These are the economic series of indicators that follow or trail behind aggregate economic activity. There are currently six lagging indicators published by the government comprising of unemployment rate, business expenditures, labor cost per unit, loans outstanding, bank interest rates, and book value of manufacturing and trade inventories.

Economic Indicators: Consumers Confidence Indices

There are two popular indices that track the level of consumer confidence: one is the Conference Board of New York, an industry-sponsored, nonprofit economic research institute, and the other is the University of Michigan's index.

The Consumer Confidence Index measures consumer optimism and pessimism about general business conditions, jobs, and total family income. The Conference Board's index is considered a useful economic barometer because it provides insight into consumer spending, which is critical to any sustainable economic upswing. Many economists pay close attention to the index, which provides insight into consumer attitudes toward spending and borrowing. Consumers account for two-thirds of the nation's economic activity (i.e., national gross domestic product) and thus drive recovery and expansion.

The University of Michigan Survey Research Center is another research organization that compiles its own index called the Index of Consumer Sentiment. It measures consumers' personal financial circumstances and their outlook for the future. The index is used by the Commerce Department in its monthly Index of Leading Economic Indicators and is regularly charted in the Department's *Business Conditions Digest*. The University of Michigan's index is compiled through a telephone survey of 500 households. *Note:* A low or decreased level of consumer confidence indicates concern about their employment prospects and their earnings in the months ahead. Uncertainty requires cautions in investing. On the other hand, an increased level of consumer confidence spells economic recovery and expansion, thus presenting an investment opportunity. In summary, an increase in personal income, coupled with substantial consumer confidence, is bullish for the economy and the security market.

INDEX